Finding Freedom *in* Forgiveness

Charlie "*T*" Jones
and Daniel R. Ledwith

HARVEST HOUSE PUBLISHERS

EUGENE, OREGON

Cover by Koechel Peterson & Associates, Inc., Minneapolis, Minnesota

FINDING FREEDOM IN FORGIVENESS

Copyright © 2005 by Charlie T. Jones and Daniel R. Ledwith
Published by Harvest House Publishers
Eugene, Oregon 97402
www.harvesthousepublishers.com

Library of Congress Cataloging-in-Publication Data

Jones, Charles E. (Charles Edward), 1927–
    Finding freedom in forgiveness / Charles T. Jones and Daniel R. Ledwith.
        p. cm.
    Includes bibliographical references.
    ISBN 0-7369-1599-0 (pbk.)
    1. Forgiveness of sin. I. Ledwith, Daniel R., 1970–   II. Title.
    BT795.J65 2005
    234'.5—dc22

                                                                    2004022062

Printed in the United States of America

05   06   07   08   09   10   11   12   / BP-CF /   10   9   8   7   6   5   4   3   2   1

CONTENTS

FOREWORD

by Ken Blanchard

I AM A BLESSED MAN.

Why?

Because, having accepted God's gift of grace through Jesus Christ, I now realize that my past is forgiven, my future is guaranteed, and my present is secure in unconditional love.

The key to all this is forgiveness—the subject of this great new book by Charlie Jones and Dan Ledwith.

For most of my life I was a reluctant believer. I believed in God and went to church every once in a while, but the Lord played little if any role in my daily life. I didn't know Jesus.

As a humanist I never liked the concept of original sin. That had always bothered me for two reasons. First, I don't like labels. If you call somebody a "sinner" they really get their back up. Second, from my standpoint as a humanist, the concept of original sin was too negative. I'd always thought that people should be considered to have "original potentiality." That is, as human beings we have the potential to be either good or bad.

The concept of original sin and forgiveness came up 15 years ago when I was flying to a conference in Mexico City with my fellow speaker Bob Buford. I asked Bob about original sin, and he said, "Let me ask you a question, Ken. Do you think you are as good as God?"

"Of course not," I answered. "The concept of God has to do with perfection."

"Okay. On a scale of one to a hundred, let's give God a hundred. We'll give Mother Teresa ninety and Charles Manson five. Ken, you're a decent sort and are trying to help others. I'll give you seventy-five. Now the special thing about Christianity is that God sent Jesus to earth to make up the difference between you and a hundred."

That appealed to me, particularly when he told me that all my shortcomings were forgiven. I'd never heard grace explained that way. Ask anybody, "On a scale of one to a hundred, with a hundred being perfection, where would you rate yourself?" Nobody would say a hundred. We all know that we fall short of perfection. What a better way to explain grace than calling people sinners.

"Before you get too excited," Bob continued, "Let me give you the whole story. A lot of people don't like the fact that Charles Manson gets the same shot at the ball as Mother Teresa, but that's what grace is all about. It's not about deeds—it's about faith. If you accept Jesus Christ as your savior, no matter what your past has been, he rids you of your sins through forgiveness, and this makes up the difference between you and a hundred."

At that conference Bob introduced me to Bill Hybels, founding pastor of Willow Creek Community Church. I asked Bill the same question I asked Bob—"Why original sin? It's too negative."

Bill helped clarify my thinking even more. He said, "Ken, let me explain the difference between Christianity and religion. The main difference is how they're spelled. Religion is spelled 'do.' That means there are all kinds of things you must do to receive the Lord's grace. Religion stresses what you need to do to deserve God's favor. What new leaf can you turn over? What new commitment can you make to get yourself right with God? The problem with religion and the 'do' philosophy is that most people quit because they never know when enough is enough. Suppose you do twenty-five-hundred good things in your life, and then you get to judgment day and the Lord says, 'That's not bad—but you needed to do three thousand.'"

Bill went on to say, "Christianity is spelled 'done.' The Lord sent Jesus to earth to take care of the whole problem. You can't perform well enough or do enough good things to get into heaven. The only entry is by admitting you are a sinner (that is, falling short of a hundred in Bob Buford's terms) and accepting Jesus as your savior. He is the only one who can cleanse and forgive your past. You can't do it yourself."

Bill talked about a personal relationship with Christ, something I had not experienced even in the days when I was active in church. "Not only can He save you but He can become your guide and your friend. He can energize your life and transform it."

The simplicity of Bob and Bill's thinking hit me. I had attended church for years, but I had never heard the message of grace with such clarity and power. All my misgivings about original sin were stripped away. I wasn't a "bad person"—I just fell short of God's perfection. And only by accepting Jesus as my savior could I be given grace. Then I could reach a hundred and be right with the Lord through God's forgiveness of my imperfections.

That realization has lit up my life so that I now have a very personal relationship with Jesus. It all began with forgiveness. Hallelujah!

May you find—or be encouraged in—that same realization as you read the pages of *Finding Freedom in Forgiveness*.

—Ken Blanchard
December 2004

INTRODUCTION

THIS BOOK IS NOT ABOUT YOU. It is not about doing versus being. It is about being in Christ and forgiven. The way of the abundant life in Christ begins with the realization of *forgiveness* in Christ Jesus. The faith of the Christian is centered on the simplest and most beautiful of all words: *forgiven.* The apostle Paul tells us in 1 Corinthians that the greatest virtue is love, and forgiveness is love in action.

All of us really have just one need: to fully understand that only God in Christ Jesus can and does forgive sin. When that tremendous, momentous realization happens in our hearts, we can never be the same; we really are "born again," "new creatures," both within and without.

We can study theology forever but if we do not begin with Christ and forgiveness, it is all in vain.

More than 40 years ago, I was introduced to a devotional book, *My Utmost for His Highest* by Oswald Chambers. I have read it, reread it, and shared it so many times with so many people that I now have most of it memorized. A few years ago I was rereading the January 10 entry, when the word *forgiveness* took on a new dimension. The scripture Chambers used was Acts 26:18, "to open their eyes...that they may receive [forgiveness] of sins." Chambers goes on to say that "when a man fails in personal Christian experience it is nearly always because he has never *received* anything"—mainly the forgiveness of sins.

Fifty-four years ago, a friend asked me to read him some verses from his New Testament. I was uncomfortable with that. I did not believe in the Bible and had no friends who did. Despite these facts, my wife got me to join a church and to be baptized with our first son. That was enough religion for me. But the name *Jesus* struck a chord in my heart and the word *forgiveness* pricked my conscience. Those verses I read caused me to begin to think seriously for the first time in my life about why I am here and where I am going when I die. When I left my friend, I was more confused than ever. I had no idea the labor pains of my new birth had been set in motion by the two most tremendous words in any vocabulary: *forgiveness* and *Jesus*. Only years later did I realize they were really one. You cannot separate them, Jesus and forgiveness.

With my head spinning from trying to put together all these new, tremendous thoughts, it seemed I was becoming even more confused. I tried to believe, but was not sure what I was to believe. I tried to have faith, but was not sure what faith meant. Yet there was something about that name, *Jesus*. Before I met my friend, I knew that I did not know God and that I had a sinful nature. But in spite of being unable to believe the verses, and unable to have faith in something I could not feel, I simply bowed my head and with no understanding, no promises, no deals, I cried out from my heart to God in Jesus' name for forgiveness. I said a few more awkward words which I do not remember, but I will never forget asking God's forgiveness in Jesus' name because the moment I prayed in Jesus' name, God helped me believe Him and gave me faith to believe. He heard me and forgave me according to the few verses I had read. Now, 54 years have gone by, and the two greatest words in my vocabulary remain *Jesus* and *forgiveness*.

Charles Spurgeon is considered by many to be one of the greatest preachers, teachers, and authors since the apostle Paul. My coauthor, Dan Ledwith, and I decided to begin each chapter with one of Spurgeon's thoughts on forgiveness. We believe Spurgeon's experience with Jesus and forgiveness as a young boy in the following story will help you appreciate his thoughts.

Young Charles Spurgeon decided he would visit a different church every week until he could find the meaning of all the great Christian sermons he had heard. Finally, that wonderful day came when a snowstorm forced him to enter a small church where the snow prevented even the pastor from arriving. God's messenger arrived—a frail, unlearned layman, who delivered a very short sermon: "Looking unto Jesus." He quoted scriptures containing the phrase "looking unto Jesus" (Isaiah 45:22; Acts 16:31) in every possible way for ten minutes and, through his invitation (which was virtually a command to "look unto Jesus"), Spurgeon realized it was looking unto Jesus plus nothing that would save him. Like Moses lifting up the serpent in the wilderness, all that was required to be healed was to look (Numbers 21:8). Spurgeon states that the moment he looked to Jesus, Jesus only, the Light of the world became the Light of his life. His blind eyes could now see and he said, "I could have almost looked my eyes away." He floated home and shared the greatest discovery of anyone's life: "I looked to Jesus and I am forgiven."

Dan and I have made the same eye-opening discovery, and our prayer is that this book will be used of God to make this discovery real in every life. I say again, life is not about doing, giving, deciding, or explaining. It is about Jesus, forgiveness, and receiving Him and His forgiveness as a gift.

Charlie "T" Jones

THE BEST-KEPT SECRET:
FORGIVENESS

*Some imagine that a sense of pardon is an attainment
only obtainable after many years of Christian experience. But forgiveness of sin is a present reality—a
privilege for this day, a joy for this very hour.*

SPURGEON, *MORNING AND EVENING*, JULY 23

JESUS HAD A SECRET. He had a secret for living and working
with people. This secret drew people to Him as to no one else.
It changed people from being thieves to being the most gen-
erous benefactors. Using this secret, Jesus replaced hopelessness with hope and released people from consuming anger,
guilt, hate, and fear and introduced them to "love, joy, peace,
patience, kindness, goodness, faithfulness, gentleness, and self-
control." This secret enabled Him to touch lives as no other
person could.

Jesus passed this secret on to His disciples, who then passed
it on to their students after them. They freely passed it on to
whoever would accept it. Many wondered what it was that

13

made so many people trust Jesus. What made Him so sought out by the rich and the poor, the wise and the simple, and everyone in between? What made people who came into contact with Him change so much? That dynamic, life-changing secret is simply this: *forgiveness—both through Jesus and in Jesus.*

That is the big secret—forgiveness? Yes, forgiveness as modeled for us by Jesus is the secret.

Forgiveness was never meant to be a secret. It was meant to be the one unique quality that distinguished Christ's followers from all other people—that they were forgiven and forgiving. Forgiveness is not a secret because it was meant for only an elite few. It is a secret because we have let forgiveness become redefined so that its meaning and power have become hidden and forgotten behind psychology, medicine, and philosophy. What Jesus taught about forgiveness is not common knowledge. Sadly, in our modern, sophisticated society, it has become a secret...a secret that was never meant to be secret.

Today there are more experts teaching and writing about forgiveness than at any other time in history, but in spite of all that is written about this simple and yet profound subject, many people are still unable to either forgive others or to accept forgiveness for themselves. Instead, we fake it by tricking ourselves into believing we understand everything we need to know about people and relationships. After all, we have learned a lot about people from medicine, psychology, and modern psychiatry. But sometimes in our attempt to understand how things work, we end up focusing on what we understand the best, while neglecting the parts we cannot fully understand scientifically.

For instance, you have undoubtedly met many people who feel they need forgiveness for something they have thought or done. Many people are hounded by remorse, guilt, or shame. They are afraid. If they could just be forgiven, they would be able to sleep at night. Their stomach would no longer be tied up in knots.

You also know people who know that they need to forgive someone. They know they *should*, but they cannot bring themselves to do it. Something always seems to get in their way, keeping them from carrying out what they know to be right in their heart. They are too angry, too hurt. They feel that the person who hurt them should pay. They reason that perhaps one day forgiveness will be possible—after the anger dies down, after the pain of betrayal subsides—but not today.

Then there is a third group of people who have trouble with forgiveness because of their moral conscience. They believe that people need to deal with the consequences of their actions. These people are concerned more with getting justice than with facing their own anger. To forgive seems to mean sweeping justice under the rug—lowering their standards, if you will. Forgiveness does not seem fair to these people.

Finally, there is a fourth group of people who want to forgive but never seem to be able to make it work. When they are forgiven, they still feel unforgiven. When they forgive, they cannot let go of the pain or of the desire to see justice done. True forgiveness seems just beyond their ability to bring about or to accept.

For the above groups of people, forgiveness remains a secret. We all have been a person in each of these groups at one time or another. If you feel like you belong or have belonged to any of these groups, then this book was written for you.

Hollywood has given expression to how elusive forgiveness is in such movies as Clint Eastwood's *Unforgiven* and Mel Gibson's *The Patriot* and *Signs*. *Les Misérables*, which deals very much with forgiveness, has been a long-running show on Broadway and has been made into a movie twice. There have even been talk shows solely dedicated to searching for forgiveness, such as *Forgive and Forget*. For all the press that forgiveness receives in America, many people still seem very mystified about forgiveness and how it works.

Jesus' understanding of forgiveness, how it works, and what it can do for us was never meant to be a secret. Our goal is to help you learn what His idea of forgiveness is and how you can start experiencing the power of forgiveness in your life, both in giving and receiving it. Each part of the book builds on the part before, so it is really best to read the book straight through to get the most out of it. The Bible is the first and last word on forgiveness. If you want to know what forgiveness is and how it works, God's Word is the only place to go. Part 1 lays out the idea of forgiveness as it is presented in the Bible. Part 2 focuses on thinking through that idea and relating it to our larger understanding of God and ourselves. Part 3 discusses how you can take that thought and translate it into action. Following Part 3, we have included a section called "Ten Habits That Promote Forgiveness."

While this book is not meant to be the final word on forgiveness, it has been our goal to write a very thorough and sound book that gives a solid foundation upon which to begin learning how to think and be more like Jesus Christ. Being thorough, however, does have its limits. What we can guarantee is that you will not find all the answers to every question you have ever had about forgiveness by reading this book. In fact, if we have done our job, you will have thought of more questions as a result of what you have read! However, we also guarantee that you will have a much greater understanding of and appreciation for forgiveness than you had before you started.

PART 1

WHAT THE BIBLE SAYS
ABOUT FORGIVENESS

1

THE WORDS BEHIND
FORGIVENESS

*What power must dwell in Him who to the utmost
penny has faithfully discharged the debts of His people!*

SPURGEON, *MORNING AND EVENING*, AUGUST 10

How MANY TIMES HAVE YOU SAID one thing and the person
you were addressing heard something completely different?
Good communication is difficult enough when we just try
talking to our neighbor or our spouse, let alone with everyone
else to whom we have to talk during the day. Many problems in
our relationships arise from simply not taking the time to really
listen to the meaning of what is being said. If there is one thing
that gets us into trouble with people again and again, it is taking
our communication skills for granted! Words are very powerful
things. They form and give expression to our thoughts, feelings,
and desires. For that reason, understanding what words mean
and how they are used is crucial to good communication.

One of the toughest jobs anywhere is language translation. Trying to carry one thought expressed with one set of words to another language with a whole new set of words, along with new rules, connotations, and idiosyncrasies, is often a long and painful process. Sometimes it is not very easy to carry over the meaning of one word in a given language to a single word in another language.

Things get even more challenging when several words in one language are translated best by only one word in another language. This is the case we have with the idea of forgiveness. There are six words in the Bible that are translated into some form of the one English word *forgiveness*. Three of these words are Hebrew and three are Greek. Understanding the meanings of these words helps us see some ideas about forgiveness that are not really implied in our English word.

- *Kaphar* in Hebrew means "to cover." This word conveys the meaning of covering up sin, hiding it, washing it away. It carries with it the idea of appeasing anger, restoring a broken relationship, and ransom.[1]

- *Nasa* is the Hebrew word meaning "to bear, take away," or "to lift up."[2] *Nasa* means to carry or take up in order to carry away guilt for the purpose of forgiveness.

- *Sallach* means "to send away," or "let go."[3] It is used to mean pardon as well as forgiveness. This word is *exclusively* used of God's forgiveness of His people. It is never used in contexts of person-to-person forgiveness.

- *Apoluo* is the Greek verb meaning "to free" or "to loose."[4] This word in its context is understood to mean to set free or pardon a prisoner.

- *Charisomai*, literally translated, means "gracious forgiveness." It means to freely and graciously give as a favor.[5] This giving is understood in terms of remitting and pardoning guilt for sin.

- *Aphami* is the Greek word for "sending away" and "letting go."[6] This word carries with it the idea of remission and pardon of guilt.

These words taken together give a rich understanding to the concept behind the English word *forgiveness*. When we forgive, we are setting someone free from the guilt of his or her actions. Forgiveness is a gracious act, a favor, or a gift. It is something that cannot be earned or demanded from the guilty. Forgiveness means to let go of our claim for divine justice. Forgiveness is a burying of debt in such a way as to make relationships whole again. It is a washing away, a lifting away of moral guilt. When we talk about what forgiveness means to the Christian, these are the broad ideas that are meant.

But definitions can only tell us so much. Definitions are short and precise. To really see what forgiveness means, we need to look at forgiveness in action, which is the focus of the next two chapters. These biblical examples of forgiveness will provide a foundation upon which you can build an even deeper understanding of what it means to be forgiven and to forgive.

2

Passages Where the Word Is Used

It is not meet that the man who will not forgive should be forgiven, nor shall he who will not give to the poor have his own wants relieved....This day let us try to give and to forgive. Let us mind the two bears—bear and forbear....Surely we wish to be blessed, and we also want to obtain mercy. Let us fulfill the condition that we may earn the beatitude....We are merciful to our fellow mortal in pence, and the Lord forgives us "all that debt."

SPURGEON, *FAITH'S CHECK BOOK*, MAY 16

Now THAT WE HAVE SPENT a little time looking at the words we translate as *forgiveness* in the Bible, let's take a look at some passages where these words are used. We have chosen to focus on three passages: two from the Gospel of Matthew and one from the Gospel of Luke. Seeing how Jesus understood forgiveness will help us form an even clearer picture of the biblical nature of forgiveness.

Conditional Forgiveness?

> If you forgive those who sin against you, your heav-
> enly Father will forgive you. But if you refuse to
> forgive others, your Father will not forgive your sins
> (Matthew 6:14-15).

There are people who think this is one of the scariest verses
in the Bible. It seems in this passage that God's forgiveness is
conditional. If we will not forgive, God will not forgive us
either. Does this mean that if we do not forgive other people,
we will cease to be forgiven by God? Such a sweeping understanding of Jesus' words in this passage cannot clearly be the
case, for the Bible clearly establishes that we are saved (forgiven) by grace alone: "God saved [forgave] you by his special
favor when you believed [in Jesus]. And you can't take credit
for this; it is a gift from God" (Ephesians 2:8).

Salvation is not dependent on what we do. In light of such
passages as Ephesians 2:8; Romans 1:17; 4:2-3; and 9:12, this
passage seems to best be read as indicating that being able to
forgive others is a *proof* of our having been forgiven. The forgiving of other people is a fruit of our own salvation (forgiveness), not the action that brings it about. God's grace is the
root that makes forgiveness possible. The fruit of His grace
includes a forgiving spirit.

In this way, the relation to our being forgiving and God
forgiving us is similar to the relationship between faith and
works. Good works do not produce or cause faith; but they
will, they *must*, accompany true, saving faith. In the same way,
God's forgiveness grows a forgiving spirit in the believer.

This relationship between experiencing God's forgiveness
and our own desire and ability to forgive is very explicit
throughout the New Testament. Many passages make a direct

connection between the two, such as Matthew 6:12; Mark 11:25; Luke 6:37; John 20:23; and Colossians 3:13. Faith without works is dead (James 2:17). If we are not forgiving, we can have no real assurance that we have been forgiven. If we are forgiving, it is proof that we have been forgiven.

The Parable of the Unmerciful Servant

Of all the passages in the Bible on forgiveness, Jesus' parable of the unmerciful servant in Matthew 18 is certainly one of the clearest discussions on the subject. The context of the story is Jesus teaching the disciples how to work with people who have sinned against them. In response to Jesus' teaching about addressing grievances to help facilitate forgiveness, Peter asks Jesus how many times he should forgive someone for sinning against him...perhaps seven times? Jesus counters by saying not seven, but seventy times seven times. He then illustrates His answer with this parable:

> For this reason, the Kingdom of Heaven can be compared to a king who decided to bring his accounts up to date with servants who had borrowed money from him. In the process, one of his debtors was brought in who owed him millions of dollars. He couldn't pay, so the king ordered that he, his wife, his children, and everything he had be sold to pay the debt. But the man fell down before the king and begged him, "Oh, sir, be patient with me, and I will pay it all." Then the king was filled with pity for him, and he released him and forgave his debt.
>
> But when the man left the king, he went to a fellow servant who owed him a few thousand dollars. He grabbed him by the throat and demanded

instant payment. His fellow servant fell down before him and begged for a little more time. "Be patient and I will pay it," he pleaded. But his creditor wouldn't wait. He had the man arrested and jailed until the debt could be paid in full.

When some of the other servants saw this, they were very upset. They went to the king and told him what had happened. Then the king called in the man he had forgiven and said, "You evil servant! I forgave you that tremendous debt because you pleaded with me. Shouldn't you have mercy on your fellow servant, just as I had mercy on you?" Then the angry king sent the man to prison until he had paid every penny.

That's what my heavenly Father will do to you if you refuse to forgive your brothers and sisters in your heart (Matthew 18:23-35).

The king finds a servant of his who owes him millions of dollars, but when the man is brought before the king to explain himself, the servant simply asks for more time to pay the money back. The servant was not asking for forgiveness of the debt, though he must have known it was impossible for him to repay. He only asked for more time to pay it back. The king shows incredible compassion by going beyond what is asked and completely dissolving the debt. The word used is the Greek word *aphami*, meaning that the king "let go" of his right to collect the sum of money from the servant.

The response of the servant is nothing less than repulsive. Happening across a fellow servant who owes him a few thousand dollars, he physically attacks him and demands his money. The very man who was forgiven of a multimillion-dollar debt is now assaulting a fellow worker over a debt of a few thousand dollars!

This second servant asks for time to pay the debt which, in contrast to that of the other servant, was very likely to be repaid. The unforgiving servant refuses to listen to his debtor and throws him in jail to work off the debt. Upon hearing this, the other servants report to the king the unforgiving servant's actions, which were an insult to the king.

In response, the king summons the servant and tells him that he had an obligation to forgive since he had been forgiven so much. The wicked servant should have been very quick to forgive since he had experienced such forgiveness himself. The king then sends the servant to jail until his debt is paid in full. Implicit in this sentence is the idea that he will never be able to repay the debt and will spend the rest of his life in prison.

Forgiveness, when it is received and realized, produces a desire to forgive other people, as we have seen in our discussion of Matthew 6:14-15. Jesus' parable also teaches that forgiveness does not do the offender any good if he does not repent to God for his offense. The unforgiving servant was fine with having his own debt written off. Who would not accept it when a multimillion-dollar debt is erased? But he had no remorse over his behavior. There is a big difference between apologizing to avoid the consequences of our actions and confessing our guilt out of sorrow and remorse for our actions.

The servant's lack of remorse revealed that he was not aware that he had done anything horribly wrong. He knew that he was responsible for a debt of obscene proportions, but once he was absolved from paying it back, he continued in the same flippant, unforgiving spirit toward other people, as if nothing had changed. His attitude thus ridiculed his master's grace and ended up getting the servant thrown in prison. Remorse over the offense is necessary for forgiveness to be effective for the offender.

Jesus ends the parable with a chilling promise: "That is how my heavenly Father will treat *you* unless you forgive your brother from the heart." Forgiveness is not optional to Jesus. The answer to Peter's question, "How many times should I forgive my brother?" is made very plain. There is no limit on the obligation to forgive. Nor is there any limit on how much Jesus will forgive.

The Healing of the Paralytic Man

Some men came carrying a paralyzed man on a sleeping mat. They tried to push through the crowd to Jesus, but they couldn't reach him. So they went up to the roof, took off some tiles, and lowered the sick man down into the crowd, still on his mat, right in front of Jesus. Seeing their faith, Jesus said to the man, "Son, your sins are forgiven."

"Who does this man think he is?" the Pharisees and teachers of religious law said to each other. "This is blasphemy! Who but God can forgive sins?"

Jesus knew what they were thinking, so he asked them, "Why do you think this is blasphemy? Is it easier to say, 'Your sins are forgiven' or 'Get up and walk'? I will prove that I, the Son of Man, have the authority on earth to forgive sins." Then Jesus turned to the paralyzed man and said, "Stand up, take your mat, and go on home, because you are healed!"

And immediately, as everyone watched, the man jumped to his feet, picked up his mat, and went home praising God. Everyone was gripped with great wonder and awe. And they praised God, saying over and over again, "We have seen amazing things today" (Luke 5:18-26).

Everyone expected Jesus to heal this man. Instead He says, "Friend, your sins are forgiven." Jesus often does not do what seems to be the anticipated course of action, and this occasion is no exception. The word Jesus uses again is *aphami*, meaning He let go and sent away the man's guilt before God. By forgiving him, Jesus took care of his greatest need: to be forgiven before God of all of his sin, past, present, and future. Understanding language is again very helpful here because English does not translate the tense of the words *are forgiven* very well. The meaning conveyed in the Greek is that the man *has been and will continue to be* forgiven. This forgiveness was instant and complete—a blanket pardon.[7]

While the crowd was wondering what to do with this unexpected declaration, some Pharisees and teachers of religious law who were there picked up on Jesus' offer of forgiveness instantly. They knew what Jesus was getting at: He was claiming to be equal with God. No one could claim to simply forgive a person of anything—only God could do that. The Pharisees were right on that fact. Only God can forgive sin (Exodus 34:6-7; Psalm 103:12; Isaiah 1:18; 43:25; 44:22; 55:6-7; Jeremiah 31:34; and Micah 7:19). The Pharisees concluded that Jesus was blasphemous because He was saying He could do something only God could do.

Jesus perceives their thoughts and brings their doubts up for discussion. "Why do you think this is blasphemy? Is it easier to say, 'Your sins are forgiven' or 'Get up and walk'?" By "which is easier," Jesus is not saying it is more difficult for Him to heal a paralyzed man than it is to forgive him. What He is saying in effect is, "There is no visible proof I really forgave him, but if I heal this man, you will have to accept that I really did forgive him." With that, Jesus commands the paralytic to take his mat and walk home.

Instantly the man is healed and leaves praising God in the presence of the stunned crowd. Jesus proves in doing what is not humanly possible (healing the paralytic's disease) that He also did the other humanly impossible thing (forgiving him). The healing is the visible proof that Jesus did indeed forgive the paralytic.[8] The fact that he was instantly healed shows us that Jesus' forgiveness was also instant. The fact that Jesus totally healed the man and did not leave him half sick parallels that His forgiveness was total as well as instant. And as sure as the man remained healed of his paralysis, Jesus' forgiveness was ongoing. It was not only forgiveness for the past and present, but for the future as well.

PASSAGES WHERE
THE CONCEPT IS USED

*And as the substitute for our guilt, bearing our sin
upon His shoulders, represented by the cross, we see the
Great Scapegoat led away by the appointed officers of
justice. Beloved, can you feel assured that He carried
your sin? As you look at the cross upon His shoulders,
does it represent your sin? There is one way which you
can tell whether He carried your sin or not. Have you
laid your hand upon His head, confessed your sin, and
trusted in Him? Then your sin no longer lies on you; it
has all been transferred by blessed imputation to
Christ, and He bears it on His shoulder as a load
heavier than the cross.*

SPURGEON, *MORNING AND EVENING*, APRIL 3

JUST AS IMPORTANT AS SEEING how the word *forgive* is understood in the context of life situations, is seeing how the *concept*
is illustrated in places where forgiveness is a central theme, but
where the actual word is not used. Forgiveness is seen in many
places in the Bible where that word is not used. Two examples
of this are Leviticus 16, where God relates to Moses the ritual

of the Day of Atonement, and the story of Zacchaeus in Luke 19. These passages are key examples of forgiveness in action.

The Day of Atonement

No day was more important on the ancient Jewish calendar than the Day of Atonement. This was the day each year when all the sins of Israel were dealt with at once before the whole community.[9] According to the directions given in Leviticus, Moses' brother Aaron was to bring four animals to the Temple: a bull, a ram, and two goats. The bull was meant to serve as a sin offering to atone for the sins of Aaron and his family. The goats were to be a sin offering, and the ram to be a burnt offering to atone for the sins of the nation of Israel.

The burnt and sin offerings were a very personal act of worship that was experienced by every family in Israel. In this ritual, the person making the offering would choose from his own animals a sheep, a goat, a dove, or a pigeon—one of the very best—and bring it to the altar. There the worshiper would place his hands firmly and intentionally on the head of the animal, signifying his awareness that the animal was going to substitute for him on the altar. Once told by the priest that the offering was acceptable, the *worshiper* killed the animal, skinned it, cut it up into pieces, cleaned it, and watched as it was burned piece by piece on the altar by the priest. This was a very personal, moving, and vivid act of sacrificial worship. It high-lighted the importance of repentance, confession, and faith in God's grace for forgiveness, and acted as a visual proof that God did in fact forgive the worshiper. In the Day of Atonement service, these rites were taken a step further for the benefit of the entire nation.

This is seen when the blood of the goat, which was offered for the people as a burnt offering, was brought into the Most

Holy Place—the place in the Tent of Meeting (and later in the Temple) where the Ark of the Covenant was kept—something never done in any other ceremony. The prominent place of the sprinkling of blood on the Ark, in front of the Ark, on and in front of the atonement cover on the altar, and on the Tent of Meeting, reveals that the penalty for sin is death.

The making of the scapegoat was also unique to the Day of Atonement. The high priest, having atoned for his own sins and having sacrificed the goat for the sins of the people, now pressed his hands on the head of the scapegoat. This laying on of hands symbolized the transference of Israel's sins onto the head of the goat. The scapegoat was then taken out of the camp and into the desert where it was left.

This tells us a key lesson about biblical forgiveness: Forgiveness is not forgetting about justice. God's justice is not ever denied. That is the clear implication of the burnt offering. Justice was never set aside. Sins are *always* paid for. God's forgiveness comes as the result of a substitution for the guilty party.

These two events—bringing the blood into the Most Holy Place, and sending away the scapegoat—"fulfill the same function from different points of view."[10] God deals with sin intimately and personally as is seen in the bringing of blood into the Most Holy Place and to the Ark, while guilt is visibly taken away from the people and away from God. The people literally watched their guilt leave the camp.

Zacchaeus and Forgiveness

> Jesus entered Jericho and made his way through the town. There was a man there named Zacchaeus. He was one of the most influential Jews in the Roman tax-collecting business, and he had become very

rich. He tried to get a look at Jesus, but he was too short to see over the crowds. So he ran ahead and climbed a sycamore tree beside the road, so he could watch from there.

When Jesus came by, he looked up at Zacchaeus and called him by name. "Zacchaeus!" he said. "Quick, come down! For I must be a guest in your home today."

Zacchaeus quickly climbed down and took Jesus to his house in great excitement and joy. But the crowds were displeased. "He has gone to be the guest of a notorious sinner," they grumbled.

Meanwhile, Zacchaeus stood there and said to the Lord, "I will give half my wealth to the poor, Lord, and if I have overcharged people on their taxes, I will give them back four times as much!"

Jesus responded, "Salvation has come to this home today, for this man has shown himself to be a son of Abraham. And I, the Son of Man, have come to seek and save those like him who are lost" (Luke 19:1-10).

Perhaps the story of Zacchaeus is not the first one that comes to mind when you try to remember biblical stories that discuss forgiveness. However, when you look closely, it becomes clear that forgiveness is a central theme of this story. Here we have the privilege of seeing Jesus live out His own teaching about forgiveness toward a very unlikely person.

Roman citizens eagerly paid for the privilege of being able to levy and collect taxes on imports and exports in their city, town, or region. These "tax-buyers" would then hire people to collect the taxes for them. In this scheme, a tax-buyer who had paid for the rights to charge and collect taxes would sublet that right to a chief tax collector, who in turn would hire people under him to collect those taxes. Zacchaeus was one of these chief tax collectors.

Tax collectors had a reputation for being extortionists because of the huge sums they collected. Tax collectors always collected more than the actual tax because that is how they made their money. Jews who were tax collectors were seen as traitors for serving the oppressive government, in addition to being extortionists. Being in such a position, it is no wonder that Zacchaeus was rich, nor was it any wonder that he was not well-liked.

Zacchaeus wanted to see who Jesus was. Being a short man he could not, because of the crowd. So Zacchaeus ran ahead and climbed a tree to see Jesus. When Jesus reached the spot where Zacchaeus was, He looked up and said to him, "Zacchaeus! Quick, come down! For I must be a guest in your home today." This was more than Zacchaeus had bargained for. Jesus Himself initiates the conversation with Zacchaeus, despite the tax collector's eagerness and even abandon in climbing into a tree to see Jesus.

All the people saw this and began to mutter, "He has gone to be the guest of a notorious sinner." But Zacchaeus stood up and said to the Lord, "I will give half my wealth to the poor, Lord, and if I have overcharged people on their taxes, I will give them back four times as much!" Jesus responds, saying, "Salvation has come to this home today, for this man has shown himself to be a son of Abraham. And I, the Son of Man, have come to seek and save those like him who are lost." That last sentence is very important, because in that sentence Jesus says to us that He was looking for the opportunity to be forgiving. He was *looking* for it. There are four facts about forgiveness that the story of Zacchaeus teaches us:

1. *Confession did not come first.* Jesus did not wait for Zacchaeus to confess or even to speak to Him. Jesus initiated the

discussion Himself. Jesus was looking for the opportunity to be gracious. There are many places in the Bible where it is clear that confession by the offender is a necessary part in the offender's receiving forgiveness (such as Matthew 18:15-17; Luke 5:32; 13:3; and Acts 3:19). A number of passages show that while confession and remorse are necessary, their preceding forgiveness is by no means mandatory (such as Matthew 6:12,14-15; Mark 11:25; Luke 6:37; and Colossians 3:13). In this case, forgiveness was the very thing that occasioned spiritual remorse. This is part of the divine power of grace. Forgiveness created joy in Zacchaeus's heart that produced not only admittance of guilt, but generosity as well. Jesus did not suggest that he return anything to the people, let alone give away his possessions, yet this was his joyous response to Jesus' forgiveness.

2. *Jesus did not bring up Zacchaeus's sins or shortcomings.* It is clear from Jesus' dealing with the Pharisees that He was not averse to discussing people's specific moral problems, but in this case He does not mention any at all. There are no words of criticism for Zacchaeus's robbing his own people to satisfy his greed. Jesus gave no sermon on the injustice of the Roman government in so heavily taxing the people, or in not assuring that taxes were collected fairly and justly. The crowd did not appreciate the fact that Christ was so gracious. It is one thing to forgive someone; it is quite another to go home and eat with a guy who had been extorting an entire region of people for years! They were waiting for the lecture or sermon on taking the law seriously, or perhaps one about how Rome's days were numbered and how God's patience with them was about to run out. Where was the prophet when you needed one?

Ironically, Jesus was sounding much more like the prophets than the crowd was willing to admit. For example, Hosea 6:6

(NIV) says, "For *I desire mercy*, not sacrifice, and acknowledgment of God rather than burnt offerings" (emphasis added). Micah 6:8 says, "No, O people, the LORD has already told you what is good, and this is what he requires: to do what is right, to *love mercy*, and to walk humbly with your God" (emphasis added). Zechariah 7:9 declares, "This is what the LORD Almighty says: Judge fairly and honestly, and *show mercy and kindness* to one another" (emphasis added).

The crowd expected Jesus to make an example of Zacchaeus, or at least make him admit his sins, publicly confess, and ask for forgiveness. However, Jesus chose not to do or ask for those things. He simply invites Himself over for dinner. Jesus was not looking for an opportunity to be righteous; He was looking for an opportunity to be gracious. He was not looking for an opportunity to dispense justice from the throne *even though He had the right*, even though He *was* right. He was not looking for opportunities to show how righteous He was, but rather how forgiving He was.

3. *Forgiveness resulted in true repentance toward God and honest remorse before the crowd.* Jesus says earlier in Luke 17:3 (NIV), "If your brother sins, rebuke him, and if he repents, forgive him." However, this is the only instance in the Bible where a word translated as "repent" is applied between people. In every other instance in the Bible, repentance is something that you do only with God. In Matthew 18:15, Jesus says, "If another believer sins against you, go privately and point out the fault. If the other person confesses it, you have won that person back." In light of these two facts, the Bible seems to be teaching that repentance is something you do before God, while confession is something you can do both before God and before other people. Jesus apparently did not keep a hard-and-fast order concerning repentance, remorse, and forgiveness.

Confession and remorse is important, even necessary for the offender, but lack of remorse, or confession does not lead to the conclusion that someone is justified in withholding forgiveness.

Grace is a very powerful thing. Grace can often accomplish what a year of commonsense sermons and lectures on moral dos and don'ts cannot. How many times did Jesus use such critical means in talking with people? Almost all His criticism was aimed at the religious leaders (the ones preaching the need for moral reform and personal purity). Think about it: Jesus was most critical with the Pharisees. He painfully and publicly revealed what they really were. Their response was hatred— hatred that resulted in murder.

4. *Forgiveness resulted in motivation for personal moral excellence.* Forgiveness was not only the occasion for real remorse, but also gave the motivation for Zacchaeus's obedience—even *joyful* obedience. There is a big difference between doing something seen as a requirement, versus doing something out of love and a desire to perform that same task.

We do what is minimally acceptable for a job we have to do. For a chore, a job, or a requirement, we want to know what we can get away with and still look good. However, we will go the extra mile for someone or something we desire or love. Forgiveness frees us *to love* obeying the law. Forgiveness became more valuable to Zacchaeus than his money or possessions. It is interesting, however, that Jesus did not tell Zacchaeus to stop being a tax collector or to give away the other half of his possessions—or that he could not stay wealthy. As the parable in Luke 18:9-14 suggests, it is possible to be a godly tax collector.

PART 2

HOW FORGIVENESS
FITS IN WITH OUR FAITH

4

THE IMPORTANCE OF
SEEING THE BIG PICTURE

*Once there was a fear of hell upon you; but now you
have no fear of it, for how can there be punishment for
the guiltless? He who believes is not condemned and
cannot be punished. And more than all, the privileges
you might have enjoyed, if you had never sinned, are
yours now that you are justified. All the blessings that
you would have had if you had kept the law are yours,
because Christ has kept it for you.*

SPURGEON, *MORNING AND EVENING*, FEBRUARY 13

*T*HEOLOGY IS NOT A FOUR-LETTER WORD.

The word *theology* comes from two Greek words: *theos*, the
word for God, and *logos*, the word for study. *Theology* means
the "study of God." We are very familiar with other words of the
same type like *biology* (the study of life), *anthropology* (the
study of people), *sociology* (the study of society), or *psychology*
(the study of the mind). You do not have to go to seminary or
have a degree in Bible to have a theology. Theology is not a

41

degree that you earn. Whatever you think about God is your theology.

Theology is important because it profoundly affects how we relate to and understand the world around us. It works like a pair of glasses through which we see the world. Our theology is like a map or a user's manual that helps explain why things are the way they are, and why things work the way they do. Understanding our theology is very important because it interacts with and informs many of our own wants, desires, decisions, and presuppositions. Your theology determines a lot about how you think and how you act.

Because theology is so influential on how we live, the specific theology we hold to is very important. It is perhaps too simple to say not all theologies are the same. In fact, no two people we know believe exactly the same way on every theological issue. Theology is never a perfect thing because we are not perfect. As Christians, we are continually refining our theology because of the Holy Spirit's continued enlightenment, correcting, widening, and narrowing of our views.

Christians who disagree on major theological issues sometimes rationalize their position by saying, "Well, I just interpret Scripture differently than you do. What should be important to you is that I love Jesus."

Theology certainly has a relational core to it. Our theology is based on what we know about the Person, Jesus of Nazareth. Theology that does not deepen our relationship with God, with the world, and with ourselves does very little good. Theology that is not able to become practical and practicable is really not good theology.

Seeing theology as relational at its core gives any particular theology's credibility a decidedly subjective side. However, to stop there would be dangerous and shallow. In order to help us know, love, and understand God, creation, and ourselves, theology must also be *rational*. Some people equate being rational with being dry and useless. We do not believe that. It is our belief that theology that is not rational cannot be *relational*. In fact, forgiveness is the key to understanding that healthy theology finds its ultimate relevance in our relationships. This is not to say that theology will ever be able to reason through all our questions, or that it will be free of mysteries and tensions. However, good theology must make sense at least in the four following ways:[11]

1. *It must pass the law of noncontradiction.* The law of noncontradiction says that any particular thing cannot be its opposite at the same time and in the same way. For instance, an apple cannot be an orange at the same time and in the same way. Any belief we have about anything (let alone God) needs to pass this qualification.

We automatically tend to disagree with or distrust things that go against this rule of logic. For instance, a university student was debating with a friend of his. At one point in the conversation this student said, "There is no such thing as universal truth." To which his friend pointed out, "You can't possibly believe that, because in saying there is no such thing as universal or absolute truth, you are saying that there is at least one absolute truth...the truth that there is no absolute truth." The student thought about that for a minute and then said, "Yeah, that makes sense, I guess."

The student's belief that there was no such thing as absolute truth could not pass the law of noncontradiction. It contradicted itself. Dr. Ronald Nash at Reformed Theological Seminary in Orlando, Florida, labels such statements "self-referentially absurd." We have never heard anyone else use that term to describe statements such as that university student's, but it is certainly an accurate description of them!

2. *It must make sense with our experience.* Theology needs to make sense with our experience of God and the world around us. Good theology is going to explain what we see and experience in life. It should explain our experience of other people. It should be clearly helpful and relevant to our daily life. For instance, our theology needs to fit with our experience that there is good and evil. Theologies which see evil as an illusion do not fit with this universal experience. Good theology will give meaning and relevance to what we see and experience.

3. *Good, healthy theology must also make sense with what we know and understand about the world and ourselves.* Theological truth should complement, enhance, and even explain other areas of truth such as science, anthropology, and history. In the same way, good theology should also make sense with what we know and understand about ourselves. Good theology should help explain who we are and why we are the way we are. Good theology will back up and explain realities such as the order and laws of nature, our need to be loved and needed, and why there is evil and pain in the world. Theology that ignores or trivializes these realities is not helpful or healthy.

4. *It must be practicable.* Good theology should be able to be consistently lived out by the believer. While no one can live out his or her theological worldview perfectly all the time, it should still be *possible* to do. For instance, atheism (the theological idea that there is no God) cannot be *consistently* lived out. The atheist cannot really claim that there is inherent value to life or that there is such a thing as moral right or wrong. The significance of life and the idea of right and wrong, good and evil, are not consistent with the view that life is a haphazard phenomenon with no design or purpose. Good theology gives answers to such questions and practices.

The beliefs that make up Christian theology are much like a web. They are all interconnected with each other. To fully understand forgiveness, we need to understand its relation to other key areas of theology it touches upon. We need to see how forgiveness fits into the big picture of our beliefs. To really understand what forgiveness is, you need to understand what needs forgiving (the understanding of sin), how forgiveness is possible (the understanding of atonement), what forgiveness reveals to us about God (the attributes of God), and what forgiveness accomplishes in us (the understanding of justification and sanctification). Let's look at these major areas of theology that have such a close relationship to forgiveness.

5

WHY WE
NEED FORGIVENESS

Sin a little thing? It put a crown of thorns on Jesus'
head and pierced His heart! It made Him suffer
anguish, bitterness and woe. If you could weigh the least
sin in the scales of eternity, you would run from it as
from a serpent and abhor the slightest appearance of
evil. Look upon all sin as that which crucified the
Savior, and you will see it to be "sinful beyond measure."

SPURGEON, *MORNING AND EVENING*, MARCH 11

AUTHOR RICHARD NEUHAUS HAS SAID the idea that everyone sins "is the only empirically verifiable Christian doctrine." We have all sinned and fallen short of the glory of God. French mystic François Fénelon reminds us that "people will always be weak, vain, unreliable, unfair, hypocritical and arrogant."[12] People ignore God, use and abuse others, and excel at being selfish. That is the way people are. If you do not think so, you need to spend more time with people! God's word for this

47

fact is *sin*. The Bible says five things very clearly about sinful behavior:

- *Sin is universal.* The Bible insists that all of us are sinners. This is assumed by the authors of the Bible as being blatantly apparent to observation. "But no, all have turned away from God; all have become corrupt. No one does good, not even one!" (Psalm 14:3). "LORD, if you kept a record of our sins, who, O Lord, could ever survive?" (Psalm 130:3). "Who can say, 'I have cleansed my heart; I am pure and free from sin?'" (Proverbs 20:9).

- *Sin exists in us from birth.* Not only is the universal wickedness of mankind shown in the Scriptures, but even from birth this is so. "Who can create purity in one born impure? No one!" (Job 14:4). "Can a mortal be pure? Can a human be just?" (Job 15:14). "These wicked people are born sinners; even from birth they have lied and gone their own way" (Psalm 58:3).

- *It is our disposition to sin.* Not only is this problem with sin universal in scope and existent from birth, but it is also described as our disposition. "An empty-headed person won't become wise any more than a wild donkey can bear human offspring!" (Job 11:12). "You are sick from head to foot—covered with bruises, welts, and infected wounds—without any ointments or bandages" (Isaiah 1:6). "She spouts evil like a fountain!" (Jeremiah 6:7). "Can an Ethiopian change the color of his skin? Can a leopard take away its spots? Neither can you start doing good, for you always do evil" (Jeremiah 13:23).

- *Sin continually worsens as we age.* This universal, innate, and natural disposition to sin grows more and more evil and continually darkens the human heart even further as we age. "And you are even worse than your ancestors!" (Jeremiah 16:12). "They go about their evil deeds with both hands. How skilled they are at using them! Officials and judges alike demand bribes. The people with money and influence pay them off, and together they scheme to twist justice" (Micah 7:3). "Just as you used to offer the parts of your body in slavery to impurity and to ever-increasing wickedness..." (Romans 6:19 NIV). "Having lost all sensitivity, they have given themselves over to sensuality so as to indulge every kind of impurity, with a continual lust for more" (Ephesians 4:19 NIV).

• *Sin has left us spiritually dead.* The worst of this condition appears in the realization that God and man are diametrically opposed to each other. "I discovered that God created people to be upright, but they have each turned to follow their own downward path" (Ecclesiastes 7:29). God says of Israel, "Yes, I will tell you of things that are entirely new, for I know so well what traitors you are. You have been rebels from your earliest childhood, rotten through and through" (Isaiah 48:8). "Their judgment is based on this fact: The light from heaven came into the world, but they loved the darkness more than the light, for their actions were evil" (John 3:19).

When we forgive, we are acknowledging a sin, an offense committed against us. Here again it is important to define what is meant by that word. What does *sin* mean? *Sin* is often defined as breaking the law of God by either doing something that we know we are not supposed to do, or by not doing something we know we are supposed to do. Ultimately, the root of sin is unbelief—unbelief in God's promises and His ability to carry out those promises, or unbelief in His place as God, or even unbelief in His existence.

It is not hard to convince people that we do not love God with all our heart, soul, and mind, and love our neighbor as ourselves. What people do not want to hear is that God holds each of us responsible for all—*each and every one*—of those failings. God's standard for righteousness necessitates that He punish all evil.

The fact of the matter is, since we have sinned against God to whom we have infinite obligations, the guilt we incur comes with an infinite punishment. Now, while it may be hard to understand *infinite*, the idea that guilt increases as our obligations to love, honor, and obey a person increases is just common sense.

If you went up to your boss and punched him in the nose, you would be in trouble for sure. But if you punched a police officer in the nose, you would be in *more* trouble. And if you punched the president of the United States in the nose, you would probably not see the light of day again without seeing bars in front of it! But, in truth, we have all punched God in the nose! And not just once, but over and over. As P. T. Forsythe says, we are not "stray sheep or wandering prodigals even, but rebels taken with weapons in our hands." It is bad enough to sin against the president of the United States of America but, as the author of Hebrews says, "It is a dreadful thing to fall into the hands of the living God!" (Hebrews 10:31 NIV). There is no such thing to God as an overlooked sin. Nothing you have done will escape God's righteous judgment.[13]

Since all people are guilty of not fulfilling their obligations to love, honor, and obey God, we are all facing the penalties for those offenses, which call for infinite punishment. Without grace, without a radical change in who we are and in our standing before Almighty God, we find ourselves right in the sights of God's perfect justice. God's way of dealing with human sin is through the atonement of Jesus Christ, and that is the subject of the next chapter.

How God Made Forgiveness Possible

In one word, the great pillar of the Christian's hope is substitution. The vicarious sacrifice of Christ for the guilty, Christ being made sin for us that we might be made the righteousness of God in Him, Christ offering up a true and proper expiatory and substitutionary sacrifice in the room, place, and stead of as many as the Father gave Him, who are known to God by name and are recognized in their own hearts by trusting in Jesus—this is the cardinal fact of the Gospel.

SPURGEON, *MORNING AND EVENING*, JUNE 21

IF SIN DESERVES INFINITE PUNISHMENT, how is forgiveness even possible? The answer is in learning that forgiveness follows justice and does not ignore it. Oswald Chambers in *My Utmost for His Highest* teaches us that

> forgiveness is the divine miracle of grace. The cost to God was the Cross of Christ. To forgive sin, while remaining a holy God, this price had to be

paid. Never accept a view of the fatherhood of God
if it blots out the atonement. The revealed truth of
God is that without the atonement He cannot forgive—He would contradict His nature if He did.
The only way we can be forgiven is by being
brought back to God through the atonement of the
Cross. God's forgiveness is possible only in the
supernatural realm.[14]

Punishment is the forerunner of forgiveness. To understand
this, let us think about what Jesus did when He died on the
cross.

There are two related aspects of Jesus' sacrifice on the cross
that we need to recognize to understand how God made forgiveness possible. First, Jesus' death was substitutionary,
meaning He took our punishment upon Himself. Second,
Jesus suffered the wrath of God the Father for our sins in His
death. In these two ways, Jesus' physical death and His suffering God's wrath, God's desire to punish all wrongdoing was
accomplished at the cross.

Physical death is necessary for sin to be forgiven, for
"without the shedding of blood, there is no forgiveness of sins"
(Hebrews 9:22). We have seen that idea in looking at the Day
of Atonement in chapter 3. The New Testament makes it very
clear that Jesus' death should be interpreted as a sacrifice
(Romans 3:25; Ephesians 5:2; Hebrews 9:26; 10:10,12-14; and
1 John 2:2; 4:10).

Sacrifices were not seen as bribes to get God under control,
but rather were offered to God as physical, audible, and visible
symbols of the sinner's repentance to God, and of the forgiveness he received from God.[15] The vivid message of Old Testament sacrifices was that they were done in place of God
demanding the life of the sinner.[16] The sacrifices accomplished

both the cancellation of the guilt of sin in God's eyes,[17] and the satisfying of His wrath against sin.[18] Both concepts—removal of guilt and alleviating God's anger—are important to a biblically balanced understanding of the atonement. Sacrifices were all substitutions for the real guilty party. The connection between justice and forgiveness is inevitable. By the substitution of life for life, the satisfying of justice is symbolized, and by virtue of the substitution itself, forgiveness was seen as granted.

If the physical death of Jesus removed our guilt before God, since "the wages of sin is death" (Romans 6:23), then His experiencing the wrath of God against sin has taken away God's anger for those sins. Jesus did not simply die on the cross. He suffered the wrath of God against sin in Himself.

This is clearly implied in His mentioning of "this cup" in the Garden of Gethsemane.[19] This cup was the cup of God's judgment and wrath against sin. Numerous passages in both the Old and New Testaments use this image of a cup of poison God gives nations in judgment. For example, Jeremiah 25:15-16 says, "Take from my hand this cup filled to the brim with my anger, and make all the nations to whom I send you drink from it. When they drink from it, they will stagger, crazed by the warfare I will send against them." Isaiah 51:17 declares, "Wake up, wake up, O Jerusalem! You have drunk enough from the cup of the LORD's fury. You have drunk the cup of terror, tipping out its last drops." Revelation 14:9-10 warns, "Anyone who worships the beast and his statue or who accepts his mark on the forehead or the hand must drink the wine of God's wrath. It is poured out undiluted into God's cup of wrath. And they will be tormented with fire and burning sulfur in the presence of the holy angels and the Lamb." This drinking of the cup of the wrath of God is the reason for His cry, "My God, my God, why have you forsaken me?"[20]

How could Jesus say God had forsaken Him? There have been many great Christians who have been martyred for their faith in the most cruel and unusual ways. But the words we hear from their lips as they were martyred are full of peace and assurance that God was *with* them. Surely Jesus, who was the Son of God, would have had no reason to say such a prayer if all that was happening was the dying of His human body. Remember, He Himself said, "Don't be afraid of those who want to kill you. They can only kill your body; they cannot touch your soul. Fear only God, who can destroy both soul and body in hell" (Matthew 10:28). What happened to Jesus was far worse than any human torture could hope to achieve. God forsook Jesus while He was on that cross.

What does that mean, "God forsook Jesus"? It does not mean that God the Father just turned His back on His Son and left Him there to die. When God forsakes someone it means that God's blessings are replaced with His curses, His love with His anger, His mercy with His wrath, His grace with the purest justice (Deuteronomy 31:17-18; 2 Kings 21:14-15; and Jeremiah 12:7-8).

The Day of the Lord, the time when God will judge all the people who have ever lived, is often used to illustrate to us the seriousness of sin to our holy God. The prophet Amos says in 5:18-20:

> How terrible it will be for you who say, "If only the day of the LORD were here! For then the LORD would rescue us from all our enemies." But you have no idea what you are wishing for. That day will not bring light and prosperity, but darkness and disaster. In that day you will be like a man who runs from a lion—only to meet a bear. After escaping the bear, he leans his hand against a wall in his

house—and is bitten by a snake. Yes, the day of the
LORD will be a dark and hopeless day, without a ray
of joy or hope.

Do you think it is a coincidence that, according to
Matthew, when Jesus was on the cross it was dark in the
middle of the day? The wrath of God was being poured out on
Christ, and the words Jesus uttered to express the horror of
what was happening to Him were "My God, my God, why
have you forsaken me?"

Do you ever wonder what hell is like? Hell is being forsaken by God. The dreadful price of sin is "to fall into the
hands of the living God" (Hebrews 10:31). Hell is the absence
of God's blessings; His mercy and grace are gone, but He is
present in righteous anger. In Revelation, the experience of hell
is described with these words: "And they cried to the moun-
tains and the rocks, 'Fall on us and hide us from the face of the
one who sits on the throne and from the wrath of the Lamb'"
(Revelation 6:16-17). Those in hell "must drink the wine of
God's wrath. It is poured out undiluted into God's cup of
wrath. And they will be tormented with fire and burning sulfur
in the presence of...the Lamb" (Revelation 14:10). The cup
Jesus was praying about in the Garden of Gethsemane was the
same cup. When we say in the Apostle's Creed that Christ
descended into hell, this is what was meant: that on the cross,
the holy anger of God against sin came in full upon His Son,
Jesus Christ. The price of Jesus giving us the precious gift of
forgiveness was His taking on the just wrath of God Almighty
in our place.

The good news of forgiveness is this: Because Jesus prayed
that prayer, His children never need to. Because Jesus entered
that truly God-forsaken place, Christians will never have to go
in. If there is one sure description of Christians, it is that they

are a people who are never forsaken by God. You can have complete assurance and peace knowing that God will never leave you or forsake you because Jesus prayed a prayer that will never be necessary for any Christian to pray ever again.

The promise of Psalm 23, "when I walk through the dark valley of death, I will not be afraid, for you are close beside me," is yours. It is your prayer, because Christ walked through that very valley and was forsaken. The great promise, "I will forgive their wickedness and will never again remember their sins" of Jeremiah 31:34 and Hebrews 8:12, is yours because God remembered your wickedness and punished it at the cross. The good news of the gospel is that though you deserve to drink from the cup of the wrath of God Almighty, Jesus took your cup from God and drank it Himself, and offers you the cup of blessing (Psalm 16:5; 23:5), the cup of communion (1 Corinthians 11:25), the cup of salvation (Psalm 116:13), the cup of forgiveness.

WHY GOD MADE
FORGIVENESS POSSIBLE

He makes the perfect garment of His life our covering beauty, the glittering virtues of His character our ornaments and jewels, and the superhuman meekness of His death our boast and glory.

SPURGEON, *MORNING AND EVENING*, JUNE 18

BY UNDERSTANDING THE ATTRIBUTES of God, we learn what kind of Person He is. What kind of a God would be moved to forgive His enemies? A whole book could be written on just that question! Let's focus on three facts about God's character that play a key part in understanding forgiveness: grace, sovereignty, and justice.

Grace

At one point it seemed rather redundant to have a section on the grace of God in a book on forgiveness. But the more we thought about it, the clearer it became that this section was very necessary. Grace, especially God's grace, is just too important to risk not being clear on.

This illustration from the life of C. S. Lewis relays the importance of grace to our understanding of God:

> During a British conference on comparative religions, experts from around the world debated what, if any, belief was unique to the Christian faith. They began eliminating possibilities. Incarnation? Other religions had different versions of gods appearing in human form. Resurrection? Again, other religions had accounts of return from death. The debate went on for some time until C. S. Lewis wandered into the room. "What's the rumpus about?" he asked, and heard in reply that his colleagues were discussing Christianity's unique contribution among world religions. Lewis responded, "Oh, that's easy. It's grace."[21]

Grace is the single attribute that distinguishes the triune God of Christianity from all other gods. No other religion is based on grace. No other religion claims a God who is known by His grace. "Grace and truth came through Jesus Christ" (John 1:17 NIV).

What is grace, anyway? How would you define it? The most common definition of *grace* is "God's unearned favor." Grace is giving blessing when what is deserved is cursing. You might well define *grace* as "getting what you do not deserve."

Mercy and grace are very closely related to each other. They are often mentioned together. It is very difficult to separate grace and mercy from each other. Both are undeserved. Both are unearned. Both are expressions of God's goodness and love toward us. God's grace is distinct from His mercy in that the focus of mercy is in not treating someone harshly when he deserves it. The difference is in the focus. The focus of mercy is relieving from trouble or pain, regardless of whether or not that pain or trouble is deserved. The focus of grace is granting undeserved kindness when, from the point of view of justice, none is deserved. Mercy removes a negative. Grace gives a positive.

God's forgiveness is an expression of His grace. "In him we have redemption through his blood, the *forgiveness* of sins, in accordance with the riches of God's *grace*" (Ephesians 1:7 NIV, emphasis added). "We believe it is through the *grace* of our Lord Jesus that we are *saved* [forgiven], just as they are" (Acts 15:11 NIV, emphasis added). "God *saved* [forgave] you by his *special favor* [grace] when you believed. And you can't take credit for this; it is a gift from God" (Ephesians 2:8, emphasis added). Forgiveness is grace in action. When you flex the muscle of grace, what is produced is forgiveness.

By its very definition, God's grace is never deserved. You cannot earn grace. Earned grace is a contradiction in terms. That is tantamount to saying a bachelor is a married man. Grace is always a free gift. It can only be accepted. This, the very definition of grace, means that its giving is totally determined by the pleasure of God. Grace is a gift that God sovereignly gives to anyone He chooses.

Sovereignty

The sovereignty of God, His being all-powerful and in complete control of everything that happens, is at once the greatest comfort and the greatest mystery to us. It is God's sovereignty that assures us that we can always trust Him. God has never said, "Oops!" God has never done anything that is second best. He is never surprised. He has never been frustrated, hurried or wrong in anything He has done.

What does it mean to say that God is in complete control of creation? It means that God has the first and last word about everything that happens, no matter how big or how small, no matter how important or how mundane. God has no need for contingency plans. He did not begin creation using plan A, with plan B ready to go as a backup. Nothing happens without His permission—*nothing*. God is in complete control.

Throughout the Bible, God is revealed as always being in complete control. Such as Psalm 115:3 where the psalmist says, "For our God is in the heavens, and he does as he wishes."

God claims He is in absolute control of everything that goes on. In Exodus 4:11, God says to Moses, "Who makes mouths....Who makes people so they can speak or not speak, hear or not hear, see or not see? Is it not I, the Lord?" Jesus says in Matthew 10:29, "Not even a sparrow, worth only half a penny, can fall to the ground without your Father knowing it."

God's foreknowledge is proof that He is in complete control. In Isaiah 45, God calls a man named Cyrus by name. God says Cyrus will be a mighty king of a powerful nation, and he is going to set Israel free and rebuild God's city (meaning Jerusalem). God even says Cyrus is going to pay for this himself. All that may not sound too impressive, unless you know that the Jews are in Jerusalem at the time Isaiah wrote this, and would continue to live there for about another 120 years! Look at 2 Chronicles 36:22-23:

> In the first year of Cyrus king of Persia, in order to fulfill the word of the Lord spoken by Jeremiah, the Lord moved the heart of Cyrus king of Persia to make a proclamation throughout his realm and to put it in writing: "This is what Cyrus king of

Persia says: 'The LORD, the God of heaven, has given me all the kingdoms of the earth and he has appointed me to build a temple for him at Jerusalem in Judah. Anyone of his people among you—may the LORD his God be with him, and let him go up.'"

Isaiah lived around 700 B.C. Jerusalem did not fall until 586 B.C., and it was another 70 years until the events in 2 Chronicles 36 took place!

How many decisions and events did God need to know about, and know for *certain*, in order to announce with confidence the name, station, and decrees of a man who would not even be born for another 175 years?

Is God in control of evil? Without a doubt the most evil thing that has ever happened in the history of the human race was the torture and murder of Jesus Christ. The reason that is the most evil act a person or group of people has ever perpetrated is because Jesus *was* the Christ. He was the Messiah, God Himself in the form of a man. No one else have we ever been obligated to love, honor, and respect more than Jesus Christ. But in spite of that, we hated Him for revealing who we really are. We convicted Him in a court of law, when we knew there was no evidence that He had done anything wrong, either in the sight of men or of God. We beat, whipped, and tore His body, rationalizing that we were doing God a favor. Then, after hating Him for telling us the truth, after convicting Him for things we knew He did not do, and after beating Him almost to death, after all that we took what was left of Him and nailed Him to a post and laughed at Him while we watched the last of His life drain from His body.

Nothing could be worse than that. But do you know what? God knew, planned, and designed that very thing to happen!

Isaiah (who lived 700 years before Jesus was born) says in chapter 53, verses 3-11 (NIV):

> He was despised and rejected by men, a man of sorrows, and familiar with suffering. Like one from whom men hide their faces he was despised, and we esteemed him not.
>
> Surely he took up our infirmities and carried our sorrows, yet we considered him stricken by God, smitten by him, and afflicted.
>
> But he was pierced for our transgressions, he was crushed for our iniquities; the punishment that brought us peace was upon him, and by his wounds we are healed....
>
> He was oppressed and afflicted, yet he did not open his mouth; he was led like a lamb to the slaughter, and as a sheep before her shearers is silent, so he did not open his mouth.
>
> By oppression and judgment, he was taken away. And who can speak of his descendants? For he was cut off from the land of the living; for the transgression of my people he was stricken. He was assigned a grave with the wicked, and with the rich in his death, though he had done no violence, nor was any deceit in his mouth.
>
> Yet it was the LORD's will to crush him and cause him to suffer, and though the LORD makes his life a guilt offering, he will see his offspring and prolong his days, and the will of the LORD will prosper in his hand.
>
> After the suffering of his soul, he will see the light of life and be satisfied; by his knowledge my righteous servant will justify many, and he will bear their iniquities.

If God can take the murder of His only begotten Son and out of that most evil crime bring forth the single greatest good that mankind has ever had graced upon it, then He *must* be sovereign over evil. There is no greater evil than what we did at the cross. But there is no greater good than what God brought out of the cross. The cross is the single greatest thing God has done to bring glory to Himself through His love, forgiveness, and faithfulness to His church. God is in absolute and total control of everything, even evil. God wants us to know that while we may not be able to fully understand how God can be completely good, absolutely sovereign, and have evil exist all at the same time, He understands.

What are the implications if God were *not* in control?

God could not foreknow anything with certainty. The best God would be able to do would be to guess the future. Can you imagine God saying, "If all goes well, My Son, Jesus, will be born of a young girl named Mary (hopefully), who should (if she sticks with the plan) be a virgin, in the town of Bethlehem (as long as Herod goes ahead with that census idea), and will live a sinless life (cross your fingers), and (if He does not change His mind) die on a cross for the sins of the world." Prophecies are simply rolls of the dice if you do not know the future.

There would be no sure hope in any of God's promises. Dr. R. C. Sproul says, "If there is one single molecule in this universe running around loose, totally free of God's sovereignty, then we have no guarantee that a single promise of God will ever be fulfilled."[22] If God is not in complete control, then maybe there is something out there that can keep us from experiencing God's forgiveness. Maybe God will not always be able to help us or comfort us or save us. Those promises that God will be our Savior, Comforter, and Help in trouble depend on God being sovereign over *everything* for them to have any real weight at all. We could not trust God or take Him at His word if He were not totally in control of His creation.

Our choices are not surprising, but rather expected by God. God told Moses before he even went in to see Pharaoh for the first time that Pharaoh would not let him leave Egypt with the children of Israel. "Then the LORD reminded him, 'When you arrive back in Egypt, go to Pharaoh and perform the miracles I have empowered you to do. But I will make him stubborn so he will not let the people go'" (Exodus 4:21). Yet God still holds us responsible. God says in the next verse, "Then you will tell him, 'This is what the LORD says: Israel is my firstborn son. I commanded you to let him go, so he could worship me. But since you have refused, be warned! I will kill your firstborn son!'" (Exodus 4:22-23).

Perhaps if this were the only time free will, human responsibility, and God's sovereignty were seen together, we could deal with this a little easier, but it is not. Judah and his brothers knew that they had done wrong by selling their brother Joseph as a slave, and believed that they deserved to be punished for their hatred of him:

> Speaking among themselves, they said, "This has all happened because of what we did to Joseph long ago. We saw his terror and anguish and heard his pleadings, but we wouldn't listen. That's why this trouble has come upon us."
>
> "Didn't I tell you not to do it?" Reuben asked. "But you wouldn't listen. And now we are going to die because we murdered him" (Genesis 42:21-22).

But Joseph tells us that God sent him to Egypt Himself so that he would be able to save many people during the seven years of famine. "God turned into good what you meant for evil. He brought me to the high position I have today so I could save the lives of many people" (Genesis 50:20).

God prophesied in Jeremiah 25:9 that He was going to send Babylon to conquer Judah for their sins: "I will gather together all the armies of the north under King Nebuchadnezzar of Babylon, whom I have appointed as my deputy. I will bring them all against this land and its people and against the other nations near you. I will completely destroy you and make you an object of horror and contempt and a ruin forever." Babylon came and crushed Judah, and sent everyone who did not die into exile. However, God says just a few verses later in verses 12-14 that He was holding Babylon responsible for attacking His chosen people:

> Then, after the seventy years of captivity are over, I will punish the king of Babylon and his people for their sins, says the LORD. I will make the country of the Babylonians an everlasting wasteland. I will bring upon them all the terrors I have promised in this book—all the penalties announced by Jeremiah against the nations. Many nations and great kings will enslave the Babylonians, just as they enslaved my people. I will punish them in proportion to the suffering they cause my people.

Jesus foretold that Peter would deny Him three times the night before His execution. But after he actually did it, Peter knew that he had failed Jesus by betraying Him when Jesus needed him most, so he broke down and wept.

Free will, human responsibility, and divine sovereignty are also mentioned together in a number of other passages throughout the Bible. Look, for example, at John 15:10, where Jesus tells His disciples, "When you obey me, you remain in my love [*free will*], just as I obey my Father and remain in his love." Then Jesus goes on to say in verse 16, "You didn't choose me. I chose you [*sovereignty*]. I appointed you to go and produce fruit that will last, so that the Father will give you whatever you ask for, using my name."

Sometimes these two truths are affirmed in the same sentence! One example is John 1:12-13: "Yet to all who received him, to those who believed in his name [*free will*], he gave the right to become children of God—children born not of natural descent, nor of human decision or a husband's will, but born of God [*sovereignty*]" (NIV). A second example is Philippians 2:12-13: "Therefore, my dear friends, as you have always obeyed—not only in my presence, but now much more in my absence—continue to work out your salvation with fear and trembling [*free will*], for it is God who works in you to will and to act according to his good purpose [*sovereignty*]" (NIV). You do have freedom of choice and the responsibility of the consequences for those choices. God is absolutely sovereign and nothing happens outside of His control.

It is helpful to remember, too, that the sovereignty of God is not arbitrary in its exercise. By "not arbitrary," we mean His sovereign power is not an unguided or undirected power. God's sovereignty is guided perfectly and harmoniously by all His other attributes. That means God sovereignly does *only* that which is also just, good, loving, holy, and wise. This is very important as it teaches that God not only exercises His good pleasure, but He also has done the very best that can be done in relation to His holiness.

Justice

God never acts unjustly toward anyone. God never does anything out of revenge. God never excessively punishes a person to make an example out of him or her. The words in the

Old and New Testaments for *justice* all mean *"keeping to the standard."*[23] When we are talking about the justice of God, we are talking about the standard set by God's moral character, His holiness. Everything God does must be just because His holiness requires it. This justice requires that all sin be punished. To ignore sin or just "let it slide" would be denying His holiness. Therefore, before forgiveness is possible, justice has to be satisfied. Oswald Chambers explains:

> The great miracle of the grace of God is that He forgives sin, and it is the death of Jesus Christ alone that enables the divine nature to forgive and to remain true to itself in doing so. It is shallow nonsense to say that God forgives us because He is love. Once we have been convicted of sin, we will never say this again. The love of God means Calvary—nothing less! The love of God is spelled out on the Cross and nowhere else. The only basis for which God can forgive me is the Cross of Christ.[24]

God's forgiveness can only be given when His justice is first satisfied. This is the radical message of the gospel: God is just in His forgiveness! Forgiveness is possible only because God absorbed the wrath and debt of sin Himself out of love for sinners. "This is real love. It is not that we loved God, but that he loved us and sent his Son as a sacrifice to take away our sins" (1 John 4:10). God's forgiveness stands united with God's justice. The forgiveness of God is freely offered to all who will receive it *because* justice has been satisfied.

WHAT GOD'S
FORGIVENESS MEANS

We are now—even now—pardoned; even now our
sins are put away; even now we stand in the light of
God accepted, as though we had never been guilty.

SPURGEON, *MORNING AND EVENING,* MAY 15

WHAT HAPPENS WHEN GOD FORGIVES PEOPLE? Forgiveness
is a supernatural event in which God decides to look at us and
relate to us through the righteousness of Christ. From our
exploration of the biblical use of the word *forgive,* we can say
that when God forgives us, He no longer holds us legally
accountable for our sins *in any way.* When we receive Jesus
Christ as our Lord and Savior, we become *justified.* To be justified means we are made *just* before God. It means that God
has restored and healed the relationship between Himself and
the believer. There are five things about God's forgiveness that

we want to unpack for you, so you have a clear picture of what His forgiveness means from what has been said so far:

- *God's forgiveness is instant* (Jesus' healing of the paralytic, the Day of Atonement). There is no lag time in effectiveness. As soon as God offers forgiveness, it is in effect. When we receive Christ as our Savior, we are at that moment forgiven of every sin, no matter how great or how small, that we have done and will do in the future. God does not think about it afterward. He finished thinking about it long before you ever thought to ask. He does not mull over how to forgive you, or wonder if it is worth His time or energy. God's forgiveness is instant.

- *God's forgiveness is total* (Jesus' healing of the paralytic, the parable of the unmerciful servant, Jesus' teaching in Matthew 6:14-15, God's grace). Forgiveness is all-encompassing. Forgiveness does not just cover past sins, or a certain number of sins, or certain kinds of sins. Justification covers all the sins a person will commit in his life. Without such forgiveness, a meaningful relationship with God would not be possible because He cannot tolerate any sin being unpunished. God's holiness requires that if God forgives us, we are forgiven of everything. To do less is to leave us in the same position of wrath that we were in before.

- *God's forgiveness is effective* (Day of Atonement, God's sovereignty, the atonement of Jesus). When we say we are justified, we are saying that we *are* forgiven, not just *have been* forgiven, not *will be. We are.* Justification is effectual, it is constant, and it is unchanging. Oswald Chambers says, "No matter who or what we are, God restores us to right standing with Himself only by means of the death of Jesus Christ."[25] The moment justification happens, we are forgiven—forgiven of everything, forgiven forever.

- *God's forgiveness is permanent* (healing of the paralytic, sovereignty of God). Once forgiveness is given, it cannot be lost. There are two reasons for this. First, once God declares you are forgiven in Christ, He does not go back on that decision. It is His decision, His choice. Second, justification is organically tied to having the Holy Spirit come and live in us, making us new creatures. Once you have been made into a new creature, you cannot uncreate your new life. Second Corinthians 5:17 says, "Those who become Christians become new persons. They are not the same anymore, for the old life is gone. A new life has begun!" God promises to save all His children. That means when God promises justification, it is His responsibility, not ours. Once God adopts us as His own children, He is our Father forever. There is nothing you can do that will cause God to stop forgiving you—nothing.

- *God's forgiveness is life-changing* (Jesus' teaching in Matthew 6:14-15, Zacchaeus, healing of the paralytic). Because justification always brings sanctification, forgiveness is always life-changing. We become different people with different wants, fears, dreams, and desires. When God forgives us, we inevitably see the world in a different light.

THE FRUIT OF GOD'S FORGIVENESS

Do you think, Christian, that you can measure the love of Christ? Consider what His Love has brought you— justification, adoption, sanctification, eternal life! The riches of His goodness are unsearchable; you will never be able to convey them or even conceive them.

SPURGEON, *MORNING AND EVENING*, APRIL 29

OSWALD CHAMBERS DESCRIBES sanctification as "the wonderful expression or evidence of the forgiveness of sins in a human life."[26] Sanctification describes the process through which we are brought by the Holy Spirit in order to become like Christ. This process is constant and ongoing throughout life and is completed only when we go to be with Christ in heaven.

The most important thing to understand about sanctification is that it is a *process*. It is a process through which the Holy

Spirit changes us so that we will have such a perfect love and desire for Christ that we will no longer sin. When we receive forgiveness, we receive a new heart. We become a new creation, a new person. In Christ we now have no excuse for sin because through the power of the Holy Spirit we have the means to resist whatever temptation we may come across.

However, our old desires are not simply replaced and forgotten. They are dying but not dead. This means that while we have the power through the Holy Spirit to resist sin, it often seems like a fight to do so. If you are feeling the struggle to resist temptation, you are not alone. You are, in fact, in good company. Even the apostle Paul struggled with this. He confesses his struggle in Romans 7:15-25:

> I don't understand myself at all, for I really want to do what is right, but I don't do it. Instead, I do the very thing I hate. I know perfectly well that what I am doing is wrong, and my bad conscience shows that I agree that the law is good. But I can't help myself, because it is sin inside me that makes me do these evil things.
>
> I know I am rotten through and through so far as my old sinful nature is concerned. No matter which way I turn, I can't make myself do right. I want to, but I can't. When I want to do good, I don't. And when I try not to do wrong, I do it anyway. But if I am doing what I don't want to do, I am not really the one doing it; the sin within me is doing it.
>
> It seems to be a fact of life that when I want to do what is right, I inevitably do what is wrong. I love God's law with all my heart. But there is another law at work within me that is at war with my mind. This law wins the fight and makes me a

slave to the sin that is still within me. Oh, what a miserable person I am! Who will free me from this life that is dominated by sin? Thank God! The answer is in Jesus Christ our Lord.

Paul's trust in God's forgiveness, gave him the assurance that grace would indeed win out over his sinful nature. Paul knew that, because he was *justified* [forgiven], he would make it through to the end of the process of becoming *sanctified*.

Jesus is not merely content to forgive us and leave us as we are. He changes us and wants us to grow through His grace so that we can be free from sin forever. "God is just in saving bad people only as He makes them good. Our Lord does not pretend we are all right when we are all wrong. The atonement by the Cross of Christ is the...[means]...God uses to make unholy people holy."[27] Every day we should be changing to become more like Christ. Part of the fruit of sanctification is seeing how much we need Christ's forgiveness by seeing the enormity of our sin. Every day forgiveness seems more and more unbelievable, while every day we also realize how much God has forgiven us.

While justification is permanent, all-encompassing, and effectual, we often still feel the pain of sin and are still instructed to ask for forgiveness, as in 1 John 1:9: "But if we confess our sins to him, he is faithful and just to forgive us and to cleanse us from every wrong." Why do we still feel guilty if we have been forgiven?

The answer lies in our point of view. As far as God is concerned, we *are* forgiven. However, as far as *we* are concerned, we just committed a new sin. When God forgave us, He saw our whole life at once—everything we are and have yet to become. When God forgave us, He forgave everything.

At this point we feel guilt for a couple of reasons. First, being made into new creatures, we are given a new taste, a new hunger for God. We begin to love what God loves and hate what God hates. When we sin, we feel all sorts of emotions like anger, guilt, frustration, and sadness because we know what we have done has offended the God we love. For that reason, we feel the need for forgiveness when we sin after becoming a Christian.

Second, we were not aware of all the sins that we were going to need forgiveness for when we accepted God's forgiveness. While God has forgiven us for all our future sins, we need to experience that forgiveness for these different sins along the way. We need to discover the forgiveness that we have waiting for us in God's grace. This is illustrated in the well-known story of the prodigal son in Luke 15:11-32.

If you remember the story, the son's eyes were finally opened to the error of his ways while feeding the pigs of his employer. He knew he needed forgiveness, but was sure he would not get it if he returned home. He knew he certainly did not deserve forgiveness. So he began the journey home, hoping only to be a slave in his father's house. However, when he "was still a long way off, his father saw him and was filled with compassion for him; he ran to his son, threw his arms around him and kissed him" (Luke 15:20 NIV). Forgiveness had been waiting for the son all along. He had been forgiven while he was feeding the pigs. He was forgiven even while he "squandered his wealth in wild living." But he did not know it. He had to discover it. He had to acknowledge it.

Just think: It was not that he did not have forgiveness, but he still had to *realize* he had it. Forgiveness was in plain sight, *but his eyes were shut to it!* Even when his father threw all dignity to the wind by running to his son while he was still far off, the son did not see forgiveness coming. He still started stammering out that speech he had been rehearsing in his mind all the way home.

When we are told to continually ask for forgiveness, this is what is meant. It is not that forgiveness will be denied if we do not ask for it. There is no way you or I could possibly know and articulate all the things we do (or do not do) any given minute that deserve to be punished by God, let alone for any particular day. We need to ask God to help us discover, realize, and experience the forgiveness that we have. We need God to open our eyes to see the gift we have already been given.

So God's forgiveness is always new to us. It is not something we experience "once upon a time," but something we experience new every day. God's grace, which we experience in forgiveness, is always fresh, always beneficial, always satisfying, and always deeper and more marvelous than it was before.

10

HOW GOD'S FORGIVENESS
IS APPLIED

*But suppose [a] man can be so changed that just as
freely as he was accustomed to curse he now delights to
pray, and just as heartily as he hated religion he now
finds pleasure in it, and just as earnestly as he sinned he
now delights to be obedient to the Lord. This is a
wonder, a miracle which man cannot accomplish, a
marvel which only the grace of God can work and
which gives God His highest glory.*

SPURGEON, *THE QUOTABLE SPURGEON*, p. 86.

THE UNION THAT WE HAVE with Jesus and the Father because
of the Holy Spirit is not something that many of us think
about or understand much. It is not something that is easily
seen, and therefore is often forgotten. There is much truth to
that old saying, "Out of sight, out of mind."

Our relationship with the Holy Spirit connects us to Jesus
and to the Father so that His forgiveness can be received and

made effective. This connection also continues through us and allows us to give real and effective forgiveness to other people. Forgiving is something that we do *through* God in a very intimate and personal way. Understanding how this works and seeing it in action can help us in believing that we have indeed been forgiven by God.

Christian faith is much more than pardon and release from captivity to sin. Christianity is much more fantastic than that! When we receive Christ as our Savior, we become united with Him. We partake in the joy and completeness that God the Father, the Son, and the Spirit all share together. Peter goes so far as to say that we "will share in his divine nature" (2 Peter 1:4). The Holy Spirit connects all Christians to Christ at all times. That is how we become and stay the body of Christ. There is a supernatural connection made by the Holy Spirit between Jesus and us.

The foundation of this union is based on "wonderful promises," the covenantal promises that God has given to His people. This covenant that God made with His people did not count on human actions for its success, but on God's own faithfulness. It is not anything on our part that obligates God to unite us with Him in any way or for any length of time. A clear example of God making this covenant with us is found in Genesis 15:7-10,17-18, where God is talking with Abraham about his future and the future of his descendants:

> Then the LORD told him, "I am the LORD who brought you out of Ur of the Chaldeans to give you this land."
>
> But Abram replied, "O Sovereign LORD, how can I be sure that you will give it to me?"
>
> Then the LORD told him, "Bring me a three-year-old heifer, a three-year-old female goat, a

three-year-old ram, a turtledove, and a young pigeon." Abram took all these and killed them. He cut each one down the middle and laid the halves side by side. He did not, however, divide the birds in half....

As the sun went down and it became dark, Abram saw a smoking firepot and a flaming torch pass between the halves of the carcasses. So the LORD made a covenant with Abram that day and said, "I have given this land to your descendants, all the way from the border of Egypt to the great Euphrates River."

This is a very important passage because in it God is saying that if He does not keep His promise to Abraham, may He—the Creator of the universe—be like these slaughtered animals! God is taking *all* the responsibility for this promise. He is not leaving any of it up to Abraham or his descendants. This promise provides the reason why God has chosen to unite Himself with us, and explains why this union is absolutely dependable.

While the reason why we are united to Christ is in many ways a "legal" one, the manner in which this is brought about is very real: We "share in the divine nature." When we become Christians, we are new creations (2 Corinthians 5:17). We are new people. We have a new heart, new affections, and a new foundation: our joy in God. We cease to be objects of wrath and become partakers of the divine nature. After this, the Holy Spirit is always at work in us to continually change us more and more into the image of Christ.

There are several ways in which this unity is acknowledged and realized throughout the Christian life. The connection is visibly symbolized in baptism. Baptism is a visible sign that points to the reality of this organic connection with the Holy Spirit. In baptism we identify ourselves with the death and resurrection of Christ by receiving Him as our Savior and Source of life. When we celebrate the Lord's Supper, this connection is visibly acknowledged again. We not only remember what Jesus did for us. We not only affirm or reaffirm our covenant relationship with Him. We actually eat with Christ and enjoy communion with Him.

We realize our unity with Christ when we pray. It is the Holy Spirit who connects us to Christ and communicates our needs and desires to Him even better than we can do ourselves (Romans 8:26). It is also through the Holy Spirit that Jesus speaks back to us. It is through the Holy Spirit quickening the Word that we receive answers, words, insights, healing, peace, forgiveness, patience, love, courage, provision, blessing, and discipline—whatever we need.

There are a number of illustrations that are used throughout the Bible to illustrate the importance of this unity. Comparison is made between our unity with Christ and the parts of a body. Jesus is seen as the Head that controls the rest of the body, but the body is made up of many diverse parts that perform greater and lesser functions that together are all necessary to have a body (1 Corinthians 12:12-31). There is the illustration that Jesus uses calling Himself the vine, with us being the branches (John 15:1-8). The strength of the branches comes from the vine. Apart from the vine, the branch will die. There is also the illustration that we are all stones that make up the temple of God, of which Jesus Himself is the chief Cornerstone (Ephesians 2:19-22). There is also the example of Jesus and the church being referred to as bride and groom (Revelation 21:1-3,9-11). Paul points to the fact that marriage and becoming one flesh is patterned after the relationship and connection between Christ and the church (Ephesians 5:22-32).

This union with Christ means several things for God's forgiveness. First, this union is what makes God's forgiveness of us possible. Since we are one with Christ, and Christ paid the penalty for our sins, we honestly do not have to. In Christ we already have paid it all.

Second, it is through the Holy Spirit that we receive forgiveness, and it is through the Holy Spirit that our forgiveness from God is made real to us.

This union is important to understanding our forgiveness of other people because it is the union we have with Christ through the Holy Spirit that enables us to really offer forgiveness. The union we have with Christ, and therefore the union we have to His work on the cross, is what provides the divine, supernatural power that makes our forgiveness of other people real and effective.

It is the offender's connection to the cross that makes receiving forgiveness possible. The work of the cross is constantly being more and more realized in the receiving of forgiveness.

Forgiveness is proof of the corporate and individual unity between God and His children. In forgiving, we know ourselves to be forgiven and acknowledge our being part of the body of Christ. In receiving forgiveness, we realize that it is our union with Christ and His atonement that makes forgiveness possible and that the power of His grace is greater than our sin.

What Our Forgiveness of Others Means

There is a wide distinction between confessing sin as a culprit and confessing sin as a child. The Father's bosom is the place for penitent confessions. We have been cleansed once and for all, but our feet still need to be washed from the defilement of our daily walk as children of God.

Spurgeon, *Morning and Evening*, February 18

THE STARTING POINT FOR UNDERSTANDING how we forgive is in understanding that we *by ourselves* have neither the right nor the ability to forgive anybody of anything. This is true for three reasons. First, since all sins involve infinite debt, nothing can be forgiven apart from the infinite grace of God offered through the work of Jesus Christ. No person can erase another's guilt before God. Second, no person has authority to judge or carry out punishment (in the ultimate sense that God does). Third, the healing that forgiveness brings is *supernatural*, not natural.

People cannot heal themselves of pain and anger. Forgiveness is supernatural in both the removing of guilt and the healing of pain and offense.

For horizontal (person-to-person) forgiveness to be biblical in nature, it must be rooted and vitally connected to vertical (God-to-you) forgiveness. This vertical connection is what gives horizontal forgiveness its supernatural qualities.[28] This connection is made very explicitly throughout the Bible (Genesis 50:17-19; Exodus 23:21; 1 Samuel 15:25; Matthew 6:12, 14-15; 18:21,35; Mark 11:25; Luke 6:37; 7:47; 11:4, 17:3-4; John 20:23; 2 Corinthians 2:7-10; Ephesians 4:32; and Colossians 3:13), and this connection is a direct result of the Christian's union with Jesus through the Holy Spirit.

There seems to be a problem at this point. The Bible seems to leave us in an impossible dilemma: The price of forgiveness is too high for any person to pay, too morally pure for it to be humanly accomplished, and beyond our limited ability to bring about. How then are we meant to follow the biblical command to forgive, such as in Matthew 6:14-15?

The answer lies in our union with Christ through the Holy Spirit. Forgiving another person means becoming the vehicle through which the experience of God's forgiveness is realized by the offended person. This is a very important distinction, because the forgiver is not forgiving in an ultimate legal sense, nor was the offender unforgiven before forgiveness was offered. This implies that forgiveness is not possible for those outside the body of Christ because the cross is essential in the forgiving process. Apart from the cross, there is no forgiveness of sins. This is the clear implication of passages such as Jeremiah 7:16, where God Himself says to Jeremiah, "Pray no more for these people, Jeremiah. Do not weep or pray for them, and don't beg me to help them, for I will not listen to you."[29]

What happens in our forgiveness of other people is the realization of God's forgiveness to the person we are forgiving. Our forgiveness is effective because it comes though the union that we have with Christ.

When we forgive, God removes our cry for justice and our righteous anger by showing us that God took that sin and hurt seriously. God judged that sin and emptied His wrath on Christ for it, taking the guilt of the offender's sin away. When the offender understands that Jesus paid the price for that sin and sees that we have accepted this, he can be free to continue in relationship with both God and ourselves. When we forgive, that is what we are doing: going to the cross and experiencing the justice and grace of God. Through forgiveness we experience the love and grace of God in seeing that justice is done. In accepting forgiveness we experience the justice and grace of God in seeing that Christ paid for our sins and took away our guilt before God and the person we hurt.

PART 3

MAKING FORGIVENESS
REAL AND EFFECTIVE

12

WHAT FORGIVENESS IS NOT

If we were what we profess to be, what we should be, we should be pictures of Christ; yea, such striking likenesses of Him, that the world would not have to hold us up by the hour together, and say, "Well, it seems somewhat of a likeness"; but they would when they once beheld us, exclaim, "He has been with Jesus; he has been taught of Him; he is like Him, he has caught the very idea of the holy Man of Nazareth, and he works it out in his life and every-day actions."

SPURGEON, *MORNING AND EVENING*, FEBRUARY 11

THERE IS A GREAT DIFFERENCE between the biblical idea of forgiveness that we have outlined in the first two parts of this book and many popular notions about forgiveness that are commonly heard. For us to take the idea of forgiveness we have been learning about and make it a habit in life, we not only need to know what the Christian concept of forgiveness means, we also have to know what it does *not* mean. There are seven ways that biblical forgiveness runs counter to popular ideas of forgiveness. Knowing these differences can help keep us from falling into common mistakes that leave us wondering if forgiveness works for us.

1. *I feel guilty, so I must be guilty.* Guilt can mean deserving punishment, or mean a feeling that we deserve punishment. There is a world of difference between being guilty and feeling guilty. Guilt has to do with relationships and responsibilities that have been damaged or have failed. Our feelings of guilt are keyed to tell us about this reality. What happens sometimes is that our memory of the guilt can be so strong that the feeling of guilt remains, even when there is no actual guilt to be feeling guilty over!

What makes things difficult is that emotions like guilt are tied to our fallen and sinful conscience. We often still *feel* guilty even after we have been forgiven. If you are wondering if you have really been forgiven because you still feel guilty, you need to take this to heart. Forgiveness removes guilt *instantly*. If you have asked God for forgiveness and still feel guilty, that does not mean He did not forgive you or that He is punishing you. Christian, forgiveness is not primarily about feelings but about your standing before God!

2. *When you are forgiven, you feel it right away.* While forgiveness is instant, feeling so does not always change that quickly. Even after we are offered forgiveness, often the pain and feeling of guilt linger after the problem has been taken away. One of the biggest reasons for this is that emotions cannot be simply turned on and off at will. The same is true with emotions of anger or hurt. Sometimes even after we forgive we still struggle with anger, resentment, and pain.

Our emotions were given to us by God to help us see and understand right and wrong. But sometimes, because of our sin, they get in the way instead of helping. There is a big qualitative difference between *feeling* forgiven and actually *being* forgiven.

Forgiveness severs the life of the offender's anger, hurt, and sense of being wronged. But more often than not, it takes a while for these feelings to go away. Forgiveness removes the guilt of the offender, but often the feelings of guilt and remorse remain. If your anger or hurt does not disappear after you forgive, that does not mean you did not really and truly forgive. This is normal! Just as feelings can mislead us into feeling we are forgiven, they can also mislead us into thinking our forgiveness is not effective.

3. *Because I am forgiven I now owe good behavior in return.* Forgiveness does not put you in debt. John Piper, in his book *Future Grace,* warns us against what he calls the debtor's ethic. The debtor's ethic works like this: If you do something good for me, I am now obliged to do something good for you. Forgiveness does not put you in debt, nor does it replace one debt for another. Forgiveness erases debt.

Grace always moves us to feel gratitude, but we need to be careful that gratitude does not become the reason for doing good to those who are gracious to us. We need to keep this in mind, especially when we are talking about God. God nowhere expects us to pay Him back with good works for His forgiveness. We need to be very careful when we say things like, "God gave His Son for you. Now what are you going to do for God?" This motivation sounds good, and even seems to make sense, but it is found nowhere in the Bible. Love for God and our faith in Him is the motivation the Bible gives for being good to other people and to God Himself: "If you love me, obey my commandments" (John 14:15). Be careful not to let forgiveness enslave you to the debtor's ethic.

4. *Forgiving means forgetting about the wrong done to me.* Forgiving is not forgetting. "Forgive and forget" is a very misleading piece of advice. Have you ever met anyone who forgets offenses after they forgive them? No! What forgiveness does is remove the pain and hurt caused by an event. It does not make us, nor require us, to forget it. Forgiveness requires us to let go of the anger against a person for hurting us, not because we need to "forget it," but because God *remembered* it. He remembered it at the cross and punished it there. You can let go of your anger because of the cross.

Neither does forgiving mean forgetting the offense by saying, "That's okay, don't worry about it." Forgiveness is not the same as letting something slide. "That's all right, just forget it" is not an example of forgiveness. Forgiveness has to do with justice being served. It is not sweeping offenses under the rug. Forgiveness is dealing with sin decisively, head-on, and once and for all.

5. *Forgiveness is something only weak people do.* Quite the opposite is true. Forgiveness is not "giving in." Forgiveness is always offered from a position of strength. Forgiveness requires strength of *character* because forgiveness requires meekness. What does it mean to be meek? Meekness is strength under control. Meekness is power under control. To forgive means you have the option not to.

It comes from strength of *position* because forgiveness assumes the forgiver is right. Remember, the forerunner of forgiveness is justice. Forgiveness is not admitting that you are wrong or that you are on questionable ground. Forgiveness comes from moral high ground. Forgiving affirms you were wronged and had reason to be angry and hurt.

6. *Being forgiving means I need to stay in a situation where I am being hurt.* Being forgiving does not mean allowing the offender to continue to hurt you or himself. For instance, a woman may forgive her husband for physically abusing her, but forgiveness does not require that she stay in that situation if it remains abusive. Forgiveness opens the door to healing of such a relationship, but the abusive husband needs to change if the relationship is to heal. Forgiveness is the *beginning* of the healing process, not the whole process. While it would be nice, forgiveness does not automatically restore relationships between persons. Forgiveness does not rebuild trust instantly. Forgiveness makes trust *possible*, not inevitable.

7. *I am forgiven, so there are no consequences for my actions.* Forgiveness does not always remove the consequences of our actions. There are two kinds of consequences: natural consequences and discipline. Life has built-in consequences. Parents may forgive their children for their wayward ways, but the forgiveness does not change the natural consequence that they must pay.

Then there is discipline. God disciplines those whom He forgives. A prime example of this is the experience David had after his affair with Bathsheba, recorded in 2 Samuel 12:1-14. God forgave David for his affair and for murdering Bathsheba's husband, Uriah. But He did not remove the consequences of David's actions and disciplined him by taking the life of the child of their affair. The good news is that David afterward is still described as a man after God's own heart (1 Kings 11:4 and Acts 13:22). He really was forgiven, even though many hard times resulted from his sin.

13

FORGIVENESS IS NOT OPTIONAL

And best of all, as the highest portraiture of Jesus, try to forgive your enemies, as He did; and let those sublime words of your Master, "Father, forgive them; for they do not know what they do," always ring in your ears. Forgive as you hope to be forgiven.

SPURGEON, *MORNING AND EVENING*, FEBRUARY 11

IF THE QUESTION IS, "Do I need to forgive?" the answer is an unequivocal yes. Forgiveness is not a divine suggestion. It is a requirement. It is a command: "Forgive as the Lord forgave you" (Colossians 3:13 NIV). Jesus commands forgiveness from His followers, and points to the unwillingness to forgive other people as a sign that God will treat you the same way. Jesus promises the gravest consequences to those who refuse to forgive from the heart. He is very plain about this: "Forgive as the Lord forgave you." There are no exceptions.

"No exceptions" is a notion that people have always had a hard time accepting. We are bent on finding loopholes, small print, anything that will allow us to be less-than-perfect in our forgiving. It was the loopholes and small print that the Pharisees had assembled around the Old Testament Law that Jesus was most upset with them over.

This attitude always reveals itself first by asking, "Yeah, but what if…?" What results from this thinking is a shifting of responsibility from the offended to the offender to make the first move. *They* have to ask for forgiveness before we will give it. *They* have to show some remorse and admit to what they did. "If *they* are not sorry, why forgive them?" we tell ourselves.

Where does confession fit into forgiveness? There are two issues that we need to spend some time on here: first, the need of the sinner to confess to receive the benefits of forgiveness; second, to not let lack of confession keep us from forgiving.

While confession and remorse need to happen, whether they precede or follow forgiveness is not the issue. The Bible says very plainly that confession is necessary for forgiveness. However, the Bible is also very clear that confession does not need to precede forgiveness. Sometimes forgiveness precedes confession. A great illustration of this biblical truth has been told in Victor Hugo's classic story *Les Misérables*.

The tale opens in a nineteenth-century French prison where we meet the hero of the story, Jean Valjean. But he is no hero when we meet him. He had been caught stealing a loaf of bread for his starving sister and her son and was given five years in prison for the deed. During his time he tried to escape and was caught, earning him another 14 years in prison.

After serving 19 years, he was given parole. At first, Valjean thought this was going to be a chance at a new life, but he soon found out there was very little place in France for an ex-con on parole. Tired, cold, hungry, and resigned to the world's view of him as a no-good thief, he is just about to give up on himself when he is met by the bishop, Monseigneur Bienvenu.

Against the advice of everyone in the town, the bishop takes Valjean in, serves him a home-cooked meal, and lets him stay the night in his home. Valjean, however, has given himself over to the idea that he is only a rotten thief. So, despite the kindness of the bishop, Valjean gets up in the middle of the night, takes his knapsack, and fills it with the very silver he had eaten upon that night, and flees.

Valjean does not get far, however. The police are watching for him and find him with the bag full of stolen silver. They drag him back to the bishop's house and present the recovered silver. What happens next is amazing as the bishop responds by saying,

> "Ah, there you are!" said he, looking towards Jean Valjean, "I am glad to see you. But! I gave you the candlesticks also, which are silver like the rest, and would bring you two hundred francs. Why did you not take them along with your plates?"
>
> Jean Valjean opened his eyes and looked at the bishop with an expression which no human tongue could describe.
>
> "Monseigneur," said the brigadier, "then what this man said was true? We met him. He was going like a man who was running away, and we arrested him in order to see. He had this silver."
>
> "And he told you," interrupted the bishop, with a smile, "that it had been given him by a good old priest with whom he had passed the night. I see it all. And you brought him back here? It is all a mistake."[30]

Then the bishop hands Valjean two silver candlesticks as valuable as everything else he had stolen put together. His story confirmed by the Monseigneur, Valjean is released by the police, who leave him with the bishop.

The police gone, the bishop hands the bag back to a stunned Jean Valjean, with these words:

> "Forget not, never forget that you have promised me to use this silver to become an honest man."
>
> Jean Valjean, who had no recollection of this promise, stood confounded. The bishop had laid much stress upon these words as he uttered them. He continued, solemnly:
>
> "Jean Valjean, my brother: you belong no longer to evil, but to good. It is your soul that I am buying for you. I withdraw it from dark thoughts and from the spirit of perdition, and I give it to God!"

The bishop's forgiveness of Valjean created the occasion for his repentance to God and changed the course of Valjean's life. His life was ever after marked by giving grace upon grace.

Another theme Victor Hugo explores in *Les Misérables* is how righteousness is often pursued at the expense of grace. This theme is seen in the life of Javert, the policeman who tracks Valjean after he breaks his parole.

Javert makes it his life's work to find this escaped convict and return him to jail where he belongs. He can only see that the law has been broken. Any good that Valjean did while he was out did not matter. He honestly believed that criminals like Valjean could never change.

Both Javert and Valjean believed they were doing the right thing. Both men claimed to be Christians. Both men looked to God for their strength and guidance. Both men prayed to God for help. Both saw God as their example. Valjean leaned on God's grace. Javert leaned on God's justice.

In the end Valjean is a hero. He grew from being a struggling, poor, angry thief, to being a mayor, a loving father, and a hero who risked his life for people in need—including saving

Javert's life from a group of student revolutionaries. Javert, focused as he was on God's justice, could not deal with the fact that Valjean had spared him. Unable to reconcile Valjean's mercy with his own view of Valjean as a dangerous criminal, Javert commits suicide by jumping into the River Seine.

This struggle of Javert's is one of the common challenges in working with fellow Christians today: the desire to pursue holiness without at the same time growing in grace. Until someone confesses, we will not forgive. When we take this attitude, we are denying one of the most powerful effects of grace on other people. Sometimes we get so caught up in being righteous—or being right—that we end up rubbing other people's faces in their sin.

Without the confession of guilt, the offender will not receive the healing benefits of forgiveness. That is true, and there is no denying it. However, there is good reason to believe the forgiver receives the healing benefits of forgiveness whether the offender is remorseful or not. God did not wait for us to repent before He sent His Son to the cross, but "showed his great love for us by sending Christ to die for us while we were still sinners" (Romans 5:8). God did not wait for us to repent before He sent Jesus to the cross. God did that first.

Forgiveness is not a license to sin. If we accept that forgiveness is one of the fruit of the Spirit, then we must also accept that repentance toward God and a remorseful heart about our sin are also fruit of the Spirit. God's requirement of repentance is what keeps us from abusing grace. People who want forgiveness to be a license to sin have missed the essence of what our new life in Christ means.

We make ourselves after what we love. Tell us what you love, and we will have a pretty good idea about what kind of person you are. We honor the thing we love. We want the approval of what we love. We praise it by embracing it. To love

God, to desire God, to have a burning affection for Him means that our thoughts, our choices, our habits, and our actions are all going to be generally geared more toward God. We want to obey God not out of a sense of duty (which is legalism), but out of love (which is devotion). Oswald Chambers reminds us, "If we try to prove to God how much we love Him, it's a sure sign we really don't love Him. The evidence of our love for Him is the absolute spontaneity of our love, which flows naturally from His nature within us."[31]

God wants us to be excellent in everything we do. The excellence of the Christian should certainly include excellence in our moral and spiritual life. We need to strive for excellence in all areas of life: physical, mental, business, home, and social, as well as spiritual. But when our striving for moral excellence begins to impede the sharing of our forgiveness, we have crossed the line.

As a matter of fact, the problem with promoting moral dos and don'ts is that this approach does not accomplish what it sets out to do: move people to become more morally excellent. Do you want to see people improve? Do you want to see people climb out of pits of guilt, addictions, and moral failings? Forgive them. Be gracious to them. Watch how fast they change.

Why is this true? *Because criticism does not work!* Criticism puts people on the defense. "But I thought criticism motivates people." Oh, it motivates people all right. It motivates them right in the opposite direction! Forgiveness and grace encourage confession and encourage opening up and being honest about our failings. One of the reasons that pornography, sex, drugs, alcohol, and the like are such problems among Christians (*and they are*) is that too many Christians are not willing to listen to people's problems in a gracious way. God never gives us discernment so that we may criticize, but that we may intercede.

The irony comes when we readily believe that *we* should be forgiven. We tend to minimize our own faults and magnify the faults of other people. Jesus spoke to this issue in Matthew 7:3-5, saying we should be much more concerned with getting planks out of our own eyes before we go around picking the specks out of other people's eyes:

> And why worry about a speck in your friend's eye when you have a log in your own? How can you think of saying, "Let me help you get rid of that speck in your eye," when you can't see past the log in your own eye? Hypocrite! First get rid of the log from your own eye; then perhaps you will see well enough to deal with the speck in your friend's eye.

Several things are of interest in that piece of advice. First, Jesus says all of us have logs in our own eyes, but everyone else has specks in his eyes—not logs. Second, while each of us needs to be concerned about the speck in our neighbor's eye, priority needs to be given to the log in our own.

We should not get so involved with seeing problems in other people that we end up seeing a speck and calling it a log. Do not spend your time worrying about other people's faults. If God wanted you to worry about them, He would have given the faults to you! You take care of your own logs.

"I want you to be merciful; I don't want your sacrifices" (Matthew 9:13). This saying of Jesus' should shock us today. Some people think their spiritual gift is "polishing people." Polishing is not listed as a spiritual gift. Fixing other people, buffing them up, and getting rid of their rough edges, is a poor use of your time. If that is you, you probably find that people you are trying to "help" do not even want to listen to you. People are probably constantly falling short of your vision of them. People are not supposed to be becoming more like you.

They are supposed to be becoming more like Jesus! Let Jesus worry about fixing everyone else. It is amazing how fast their problems get fixed when you start focusing on your own shortcomings and failings.

14

FORGIVING YOURSELF

*And now it is my unceasing joy to know that my sins
are no longer imputed to me but are laid on Him. Like
the debts of the wounded traveler, Jesus, like the good
Samaritan, has said of all my future sinfulness, "Set
that to My account." Blessed discovery! Eternal solace
of a grateful heart!*

SPURGEON, *MORNING AND EVENING*, APRIL 13

$\mathbf{W}$E HAVE ALL DONE THINGS that we feel horrible about in
retrospect. Many of us have felt that what we need is to forgive
ourselves.

There is one problem with that: There is not one scripture
that addresses forgiving yourself! The Bible is full of passages
about how God can and does forgive people. It also has a lot to
say about our forgiving *other* people. But there is no verse or
passage in the Bible that has to do with forgiving yourself.
That leads to the questions, "Can you forgive yourself? What
do you do when you feel that is what you need to do?"

Certainly there are examples of people in the Bible who have felt like they needed forgiveness for their own sanity. David, for instance, wrote a number of psalms that tell of his own struggle with such feelings. A great example is Psalm 38. David wrote this psalm at a time when he felt overridden with guilt and was looking for relief. Listen to his words. We have all identified with them at one point or another:

> O Lord, don't rebuke me in your anger!
> Don't discipline me in your rage!
> Your arrows have struck deep, and your blows are
>   crushing me.
> Because of your anger, my whole body is sick;
>   my health is broken because of my sins.
> My guilt overwhelms me—
>   it is a burden too heavy to bear.
> My wounds fester and stink
>   because of my foolish sins.
> I am bent over and racked with pain.
> My days are filled with grief.
> A raging fever burns within me,
>   and my health is broken.
> I am exhausted and completely crushed.
> My groans come from an anguished heart.
> You know what I long for, Lord;
>   you hear my every sigh.
> My heart beats wildly, my strength fails,
>   and I am going blind.
> My loved ones and friends stay away, fearing my
>   disease.
> Even my own family stands at a distance.
> Meanwhile, my enemies lay traps for me;
>   they make plans to ruin me.
> They think up treacherous deeds all day long.

But I am deaf to all their threats.
I am silent before them as one who cannot speak.
I choose to hear nothing,
     and I make no reply.
For I am waiting for you, O LORD.
You must answer for me, O Lord my God.
I prayed, "Don't let my enemies gloat over me
     or rejoice at my downfall."
I am on the verge of collapse,
     facing constant pain.
But I confess my sins;
     I am deeply sorry for what I have done.
My enemies are many;
     they hate me though I have done nothing to
     them.
They repay me evil for good
     and oppose me because I stand for the right.
Do not abandon me, LORD.
Do not stand at a distance, my God.
Come quickly to help me, O Lord my savior.

Guilt can make you feel this way. It can eat away at your soul and infect your body. Our failures, sins, and shortcomings can stop us in our tracks. While no one knows what event or events preceded this psalm, there are four things we can get from it that can help us when we are feeling this way.

1. *David felt like God was against him.* Does God still "punish" us for sin after He has forgiven us? Jesus Christ has paid for sin at the cross. There is no reason for God to "punish" His children. God's punishment has been spent. But God still *disciplines* us. In Hebrews 12:5-11 we are told,

And have you entirely forgotten the encouraging words God spoke to you, his children? He said,

> "My child, don't ignore it when the Lord
>   disciplines you,
> and don't be discouraged when he corrects you.
> For the Lord disciplines those he loves,
> and he punishes[32] those he accepts as his
>   children."

As you endure this divine discipline, remember that God is treating you as his own children. Whoever heard of a child who was never disciplined? If God doesn't discipline you as he does all of his children, it means that you are illegitimate and are not really his children after all. Since we respect our earthly fathers who disciplined us, should we not all the more cheerfully submit to the discipline of our heavenly Father and live forever?

For our earthly fathers disciplined us for a few years, doing the best they knew how. But God's discipline is always right and good for us because it means we will share in his holiness. No discipline is enjoyable while it is happening—it is painful! But afterward there will be a quiet harvest of right living for those who are trained in this way.

"What is the difference?" you say. "Aren't punishing and disciplining the same?" There is a difference, but the popular idea of discipline has been given a very negative connotation. Discipline is perceived as negative, as something that keeps us from doing what we want to do. Personal choice and freedom from the judgment of other people are two of the ideas in our culture that have taken away any positive power the proper idea of discipline should convey.

The author of Hebrews gives us a clue to the true meaning of discipline here in verse 11. There is a parallel made between discipline and training. Think of seeing God as the coach and each of us as members of His team. Everyone has the will to win, but not everyone has the will to *prepare* to win. Before you play the game, you need to be trained. Training is hard. It can be strenuous. It is often monotonous. It sometimes makes you wonder if you are nuts for going through such pain and agony.

Heavyweight champion boxer Evander Holyfield talks about how the training he went through to get ready for a fight was so grueling and draining that the fight was easy. To win it took the willingness to accept the discipline of his coach. He had to be willing to do the necessary training so that when the event came, he would be well-prepared.

That is what discipline means in Psalm 38:1 and Hebrews 12:5-11. Discipline is God training us, changing us, and getting us ready for the things He has prepared in advance for us to do. God uses our mistakes, our sins, our failings, and our struggles to make us better people, to make us more like Him, to make His ministry through us more powerful.

2. *David felt overwhelmed by the situation.* Guilt can do that to us. Feelings of guilt can actually make us physically ill. David did not think he could take the pressure much longer. His guilt brought depression, fear, and illness. His guilt left him bedridden. This is what can happen when we cannot get our eyes off our failures. What makes the difference in these times is how we respond to them. Oswald Chambers reminds us about this fact: "If we were never depressed, we would not be alive. If human beings were not capable of depression, we would have no capacity for happiness and exultation."[33]

One of the keys to having a healthy attitude during overwhelming circumstances is in understanding that our experience is not unique. All of us have gone through times of such pain and agony that we wondered whether we would make it to tomorrow—and most of us will experience such times again! One of the most important lessons to remember in times like these is from the story of Job.

Job was a righteous man who sought after God's own heart. God Himself says there was no one else like him on the face of the earth (Job 1:8). And then, for no humanly discernible reason, everything Job valued—everything Job had worked for, and prayed for, and fought for—was gone, just like that. The man of God of whom there was no equal on earth, that blameless and upright man, was left sitting in a pile of coarse ashes scraping at himself with a dirty shard of broken pottery saying, "What I always feared has happened to me. What I dreaded has come to be. I have no peace, no quietness. I have no rest; instead, only trouble comes" (Job 3:25-26).

The story of Job teaches many things, but perhaps the most important lesson is this: Job is not the exception—he is the *rule*. We often think of Job's experience as something God does only to people with extraordinary faith who can handle such trauma. But God did not put that huge 40-chapter book right in the middle of the Bible so that a few of us who really struggle and suffer have a little word from God on how to cope. Job is *not* the exception—he is the *rule!*

All God's great leaders go through valleys of disappointments, pain, betrayals, suffering, and loneliness—deep and lonely valleys. Before he was king, David had to run for his life and hide in a cave. Abraham had to give up Isaac. Moses had to run for his life and live in the desert for 40 years. Joseph was beaten, betrayed, and sold as a slave. Jeremiah remained lonely his whole life. Jonah was thrown into the sea and swallowed by a giant sea creature. Daniel was thrown in the lions' den; his friends were thrown into the fiery furnace. Jesus took on the wrath of His Father for the sins of the entire world. Job is not the exception—he is the rule!

All God's children experience times like these. Life is not designed to be a bed of roses. Being a Christian does not make these painful times go away. Quite the opposite is true, in fact. There is one thing you can know with absolute certainty about your future: There will be times in your life when you will feel like things cannot possibly get worse, *and then they will!*

What is the point of these hard times? They are to build you and mold you and change you into the man or woman God knows you to be. The purest gold is the gold refined by the fire. The reason for a crucible is to purify, to make better, to increase worth. The most beautiful glass is the glass that has been heated and blown while in the heat of the fire.

A vivid example of this is from the movie *The Prince of Egypt*. One of most moving scenes in that movie is when Moses encounters the burning bush. The fantastic thing about this scene is the fact that the bush is growing, blooming, even flourishing in the fiery presence of God. We often think of fire as a bad thing, as something destructive. But something happens when God gets ahold of fire. It becomes life-giving.

These painful events, which we might be tempted to think are the end of us, become the very things that build our perseverance, character, and hope. "We can rejoice, too, when we run into problems and trials, for we know that they are good for us—they help us learn to endure. And endurance develops strength of character in us, and character strengthens our confident expectation of salvation" (Romans 5:3-4). Trials are the very things that make us the people we want to become. Think about it: How many people do you know and look up to that did not come through some terrible low point in their life? The greatest people, the wisest people, the people we all want to become, the people we most admire—these are the people who have failed the most, hurt the worst, been rejected the most, and had the most disappointments. Be prepared. Life is going to knock you down. God says to get back up.

3. *David felt responsible for getting himself in his painful position.* David acknowledged that *his* choices and *his* sins had, in many ways, brought him to where he was (Psalm 38:4,18). David knew he was responsible for his own actions. The positions and circumstances we find ourselves in are almost often times a direct result of past choices.

This is one of the things that made David great: his willingness to take responsibility for his failures. David acknowledged that the guilt he was feeling was his own fault. He *deserved* the consequences. He was responsible and culpable for his sins.

When we feel this way about ourselves, we need to do what David did and take responsibility for our actions. Making excuses and blaming circumstances does not help; in fact, it does just the opposite. Instead of preparing us to move on, it conditions us to accept the lie that there is no way for us to get out from under the grasp of sin. That is not the message of grace and forgiveness. We are free of that. "For I can do everything with the help of Christ who gives me the strength I need" (Philippians 4:13).

4. *David looked to God's grace for relief, not to himself.* In this situation, overcome with grief for his sins and failures, agonizing under the weight of his circumstances, David did not look to forgive himself. He looked to God for forgiveness. It is important to remember that David was not afraid to tell God how he felt. Certainly there was confession. He knew that in many ways he had brought this trouble on himself, but he felt free to vent his frustrations and hurt to God. He trusted that

God would forgive him. He not only trusted that God would forgive him, he also trusted that God's grace would bring him through to the other side of his suffering. God was the Source of the grace he needed. God was the Person he had offended. Only God can remove real guilt.

Our attitude here is crucial. This is one of Satan's biggest traps: keeping us in the prison of guilt when the door has been unlocked, swung open, and we are free to leave. It is at this point that we either grow from the experience or define ourselves by that experience. Oswald Chambers writes about such situations in *My Utmost for His Highest:*

> Depression tends to turn us away from the everyday things of God's creation. But whenever God steps in, His inspiration is to do the most natural, simple things—things we would never have imagined God was in, but as we do them we find Him there. The inspiration that comes to us in this way is an initiative against depression. But we must take the first step and do it in the inspiration of God. If, however, we do something simply to overcome our depression, we will only deepen it. But when the Spirit of God leads us instinctively to do something, the moment we do it the depression is gone. As soon as we arise and obey, we enter a higher plane of life.[34]

When we forget the fact that we have been forgiven and focus instead on our failures, we are robbing ourselves of the freedom God's forgiveness has purchased for us. When feelings of guilt are overcoming us, the solution does not lie in becoming fixated on our feelings or on the situation or on how we got there, but in doing the next right thing. There is nothing wrong in examining past failures and sins to find what caused us to do those things so that we can avoid them in the future. That is healthy. What we do not want to do is become fixated on them so that we never move on.

When we feel like we need to forgive ourselves, what we really need (if we are honest with ourselves) is God's forgiveness for ourselves. Remember, forgiveness is a divinely powered action. You cannot forgive yourself by yourself. You need God to forgive you. Perhaps the real challenge comes when the situation, the feelings, and the pain do not simply disappear after God forgives us.

Often feelings of guilt linger, and we still feel the need to be forgiven. We still feel like we must somehow do something to redeem ourselves. We cannot believe that we actually have been forgiven. The issue here is not how to forgive ourselves, but needing to accept the fact that we already have been forgiven. Christ has paid for our sins. God has accepted that payment. We are free from guilt. There is nothing left to do or pay.

15

WHEN ANGER KEEPS US FROM FORGIVING

The only weapon to fight sin with is the spear that pierced the side of Jesus. To give an illustration—if you want to overcome an angry temper, how do you go about it? It is very possible that you have never tried the right way of going to Jesus with it. How did I get my salvation? I came to Jesus just as I was, and I trusted Him to save me. I must kill my angry temper in the same way. It is the only way in which I can ever kill it. I must go to the cross with it and say to Jesus, "Lord, I trust You to deliver me from it."

SPURGEON, *MORNING AND EVENING*, APRIL 23

W<small>E SOMETIMES LET OUR ANGER</small> get in the way of forgiveness. What can we do to get over our anger?

The first thing we need to think about when anger keeps us from forgiving is that at this point our anger is no longer doing what it is supposed to do. When anger gets divorced from love for other people, anger ceases to be righteous. Anger is designed to let us know we have been treated unjustly or when we have seen someone else treated unjustly, that someone has been wronged. Anger is a cry for justice, a cry for sin to be recognized for what it is and punished accordingly.

Removing righteous anger is one of the supernatural effects of forgiveness. If we want to get rid of the anger, the solution lies in forgiveness! But what if when we really get honest with ourselves, we do not *want* to get rid of anger? What if we want to stay angry?

If this is the case, we need to ask the question, "Am I really feeling *righteous* anger?" The affection of anger leaves us in control of ourselves rationally. When anger keeps us from doing what we know we should be doing, we are no longer dealing with anger but with something else. We have crossed over the line from affection to a passion, to a feeling that controls our thoughts and actions more than our minds.

One of two things is happening here: We are either being controlled by our feelings, or we are being controlled by another person. More accurately, we should say we are *allowing* ourselves to be controlled by our emotions or another person. We need to accept that if our emotions are out of our control and are blocking us from doing what we know to be right, *we* are sinning and need forgiveness ourselves.

God addressed this very situation with Jonah. Jonah was told by God to go and preach to the city of Nineveh. Nineveh was the capital of the Assyrian Empire. Assyria was a great and powerful nation. The Assyrians could be ruthless in war. Even cities that surrendered to them had their inhabitants carried off with nose rings and hooks into exile. They were the enemy, and God told Jonah to go and preach to them.

He refused to go. To make his feelings perfectly clear, he ran off in the opposite direction. Jonah ran because he was afraid, but not afraid of what you might think. Jonah was not running because he was afraid of the Assyrians. He was a zealous Jew and a patriot. He was afraid of God's grace! He was afraid of God's grace being offered to his pagan enemy.

It turns out that Jonah had good reason to be afraid. Despite the blunt doom-and-gloom proclamation of the prophet, the Ninevites took the chance that God might not destroy them if they repented. They did repent, and God did not destroy them. When Jonah realized this, he became exceedingly angry. He was so angry, in fact, that he wanted to die rather than watch this city receive any amount of God's grace. Jonah was so angry with God and with the people of Nineveh that he could not—he would not—join God in being happy that they repented. In the opening verses of Jonah 4 we read,

> This change of plans upset Jonah, and he became very angry. So he complained to the LORD about it: "Didn't I say before I left home that you would do this, LORD? That is why I ran away to Tarshish! I knew that you were a gracious and compassionate God, slow to get angry and filled with unfailing love. I knew how easily you could cancel your plans for destroying these people. Just kill me now, LORD! I'd rather be dead than alive because nothing I predicted is going to happen."

God's immediate response to Jonah was to question the credibility of his anger. In verse 4, God replies, "Is it right for you to be angry about this?" The answer in Jonah's case was obviously no. When anger keeps us from forgiving, we need to ask ourselves that same question: "Is my anger really justified?"

One of the most important things to talk about in making forgiveness real and effective is to understand the role that certain affections play in forgiveness. Let's take a minute or two to define what we mean by *affection*. An affection is one of three levels of emotion[35]:

1. *Feelings*. Feelings are low-level emotions. There may be a better word out there for this class of emotion than *feelings* and when we find it we will change this word. Feelings are emotions we have which do not really have any long-term effect on us or on the way we think. They come and go; they are not permanent. Some examples of feelings are like, dislike, annoyance, sadness, and happiness.

2. *Affections*. Affections are stronger emotions that tend to affect the way we physically feel. Affections send chills down our spines and stand the hair up on the back of our necks. Affections make our hearts beat faster and leave our mouths dry. Affections are called affections because they really physically *affect* us. Affections, while they are very strongly felt by us in many ways, do not shut off our thinking and rational selves. They tend to not fade and come back, but are permanent. Examples of affections are love, hate, anger, grief, and joy.

3. *Passions*. Passions are extremely heightened emotions that not only affect us physically, but also tend to override our ability to think about what we are doing. When passions are in control, the mind is not. We are not thinking about the consequences our actions might have. Examples of passions are lust, loathing, rage, depression, and ecstasy.

This is probably a good point to say that anger is not a bad or wrong affection in and of itself. Anger is part of the image of God in us. Anger, when it is legitimate, should motivate us to action. It should bring us closer to Christ and compel us to boldly witness for Him. Anger is sinful when it takes us away from God and takes away our love for our neighbors.

A forgiving spirit is a sign that we have been forgiven ourselves. When we persist over time with an unforgiving spirit, it is a sign that, at best, we need to seek serious spiritual help. At worst, our own state of forgiveness before God may need to be questioned. That is a very strong statement. You might need to read that again. An unforgiving spirit is a very grave spiritual issue.

If Jonah was an example of allowing anger to impede forgiveness, Joseph is a great example of overcoming anger to offer forgiveness. He is a great example to us about controlling our anger. Joseph's own hurt and anger welled up even after 20 years had gone by without seeing the brothers that beat him up, threw him into a pit, and sold him into slavery. In his anger, Joseph threw his brothers in prison for three days (Genesis 42:17). Joseph's anger was not aimed at exacting revenge; rather, it was aimed at bringing about confession and remorse for their sin.

Joseph saw his brothers through God's grace. Their pain and struggle with what they had done to him brought Joseph to tears (Genesis 42:24). Seeing them as his brothers, as people in need of God's grace, moved him from anger and suspicion to forgiveness.

Joseph remembered the grace of God and found the strength to forgive his brothers. When anger keeps us from forgiving, we need to go to the cross. The cross is God's concrete example of grace in action. We need to look at the other person through the cross. Anger is a call for justice, and looking through the cross we see that God dealt with the sin of the offender decisively. We see that God the Father took that sin, that injury to us, so seriously that He came on His Son in the fullness of His wrath. Justice has been done. Seeing that our anger was heard and answered by God the Father at the cross, the Holy Spirit can remove our anger.

Joseph saw a bigger picture of himself through God's grace. Joseph saw and understood that it was not his place to judge his brothers. That was God's job, and God's job alone. "Don't be afraid of me. Am I God, to judge and punish you?" (Genesis 50:19). At the cross we see ourselves. We remember how much God has forgiven us. Again, the parable of the unmerciful servant in Matthew 18 is key in helping us understand this supernatural event. The cross has done as much for those who have offended us as it has for us. Anything that we forgive is merely a fraction of what God has forgiven any one of us for.

16

WHEN CONSCIENCE KEEPS US FROM FORGIVING

Nothing is more deadly than self-righteousness or more powerful than contrition.

SPURGEON, *MORNING AND EVENING,* FEBRUARY 26

ARE THERE EVER INSTANCES when we are justified in withholding forgiveness out of concern for justice? That question seems to limit the sins for which Christ died. If there are such instances, we cannot think of any. Remember, forgiveness is only possible because justice has already been met at the cross. No one gets away with anything. Every sin is paid for. Every sin brings the full and undiluted wrath of God. What can we do to keep our sense of justice from impeding our willingness and ability to forgive?

First, we must remember how much we have been forgiven. We always give ourselves more slack than we are willing to give other people. We need to treat other people the way we want to be treated. Notice that we did not say treat people the way they treat us, but treat people the way we want to be treated in the same circumstance. "Do for others what you would like them to do for you. This is a summary of all that is taught in the law and the prophets" (Matthew 7:12).

Second, ask yourself this question: "Is my withholding forgiveness an act of love which intends to bring that person or persons back into fellowship with me or to a saving knowledge of Christ?" If your answer is no, then you need to rethink your position. Remember Jesus' promise at the end of the parable in Matthew 18:34-35: "Then the angry king sent the man to prison until he had paid every penny. That's what my heavenly Father will do to you if you refuse to forgive your brothers and sisters in your heart."

Third, pray before you take any kind of action. Talk to your pastor or counselor before you do anything that might make things worse instead of better. Our desire to see justice done right away can often be an extremely powerful emotion. Taking time to think over what you want to do by taking your thoughts to God and other people will keep you from simply reacting to the situation. You want to respond, not react. When you react, the situation is controlling you. When you respond, you are controlling your actions in light of the situation.

The Church (the body of Christ) has been divinely called and set apart by God to be the standard of righteousness in the world. The Church cannot—*must not*—abandon this mission. However, when we pursue this at the expense of forgiveness, our righteousness means little. Jesus' criticism of the Pharisees is just as much aimed at many of us today:

> How terrible it will be for you teachers of religious law and you Pharisees. Hypocrites! For you are careful to tithe even the tiniest part of your income,

but you ignore the important things of the law—justice, mercy, and faith. You should tithe, yes, but you should not leave undone the more important things. Blind guides! You strain your water so you won't accidentally swallow a gnat; then you swallow a camel! (Matthew 23:23-24).

If you were to name all the persons in your life who excel at grace, chances are you would not need more than the fingers of both hands to count them. But we cannot even begin to count the people we know who excel at being right! As the story of Zacchaeus shows us, the irony is that in emphasizing grace and sincere forgiveness, we promote the righteousness we seek.

Perhaps one of the strongest reasons that we should not allow our desires for justice to keep us from forgiving is that life has a way of dishing out its own rewards and consequences. You might even say life is not very forgiving. Life has a way of making people pay the price for what they do. This is all the more reason we should be forgiving. People are going to be reprimanded by somebody. Let us be gracious and forgiving.

Both approaches (bringing to justice and offering forgiveness) have the same goal in mind. Both approaches start with compassion and love for other people. But one is much more effective than the other. When we focus on getting other people to be right instead of excelling at being gracious, we are in effect treating the symptoms and not the disease. The problem of more and more Christians struggling with immorality, anger, strife, and contention is not a sign we need to talk more about what people need to do right. It is a sign that we need more teaching on Christ's forgiveness.

This means learning to love the sinner while hating the sin. That can be a very hard thing to do. Or is it? C. S. Lewis helps us understand how to go about doing that—simply by treating people the way we treat ourselves:

> For a long time I used to think this a silly, straw-splitting distinction: how could you hate what a man did and not hate the man? But years later it occurred to me that there was one man to whom I had been doing this all my life—namely myself. However much I might dislike my own cowardice or conceit or greed, I went on loving myself. There had never been the slightest difficulty about it. In fact the very reason why I hated the things was that I loved the man. Just because I loved myself, I was sorry to find that I was the sort of man who did those things. Consequently, Christianity does not want us to reduce by one atom the hatred we feel for cruelty and treachery. We ought to hate them....But it does want us to hate them in the same way in which we hate things in ourselves: being sorry that the man should have done such things, and hoping, if it is anyway possible, that somehow, sometime, some-where, he can be cured and made human again.[36]

When grace comes, righteousness immediately follows through and in Christ. Again, we must not abandon our commitment to truth and justice. We need to be preaching, living, teaching, and giving the truths of grace and forgiveness. There is a difference between compassionate righteousness (grace and truth) and judgmental righteousness. "For the law was given through Moses; grace and truth came through Jesus Christ" (John 1:17 NIV). How important is the order of those words? Notice it is grace *then* truth—truth surrounded by grace. Truth without grace leads to hopelessness. Truth with grace frees us to embrace and love the Truth, Jesus Christ.

TEN HABITS THAT
PROMOTE FORGIVENESS

If we have received Christ himself in our innermost hearts, our new life will manifest its intimate acquaintance with him by a walk of faith in him. Walking implies action. Our religion is not to be confined to our closet; we must carry out into practical effect that which we believe. If a man walks in Christ, then he acts as Christ would act; for Christ being in him, his hope, his love, his joy, his life, he is the reflex of the image of Jesus; and men say of that man, "He is like his Master; he lives like Jesus Christ."

SPURGEON, *MORNING AND EVENING*, NOVEMBER 9

THERE ARE MANY BOOKS OUT THERE on forgiveness, but there are few books that offer practical help on how we can become more forgiving people. Forgiveness is not something that comes naturally to any of us. It has to be experienced, realized, cultivated, and practiced. Forgiveness, like any other fruit of the Spirit, grows well in some environments and struggles in others. Being forgiving means thinking in certain ways, feeling certain affections, and having certain attitudes. It also means getting rid of certain thoughts, affections, and attitudes that hinder forgiveness.

These three things—thoughts, affections, and attitudes—determine the way we act. It is important to accept this truth if you are interested in becoming a more forgiving person. It is important because changing anything else is not going to produce results! God has made it very clear in the Scriptures that our growth in Christ is determined by what we think about. The key to real change and growth is in changing the way you think about who you are in Christ because of His forgiveness.

Why should you change? Why should you be willing to do all the hard work that it takes to be a more forgiving person? That is a good question. And if you have not asked yourself that question yet, you need to. Unless you have a clear motivation to change, you will not go to the trouble. You need reasons to change—good, God-honoring reasons to change. Take some time to write down three reasons why you want to become a more forgiving person and read them every morning and every evening until you have grown into the description you wrote down.

God's grace is not cheap. It cost Him His Son. Forgiveness is not cheap for us, either. We may not be paying the price to purchase forgiveness, but we still have to pay a price to practice it. Being forgiving is not easy, but the rewards that come with it far outweigh the price of developing a forgiving spirit.

What follows are ten habits that anyone can learn in order to become a more forgiving person. And when we say anyone, we mean *anyone!* You will notice that these ten habits are of three kinds: habits of thought, habits of affection, and habits of action. These habits will take work to bring them about, but you *can* make them a part of your life! In fact, we are certain that if you persist, no matter how many setbacks and mistakes and stumbles you may make, you will make these ten habits a reality.

1. Cultivate Affection and Desire for God

One of the key ideas throughout this book has been the connection that exists between vertical (God to you) forgiveness and horizontal (person to person) forgiveness. Because of that connection, this first habit will help greatly in your working at the other nine. Why? Because everything that follows is really an extension of this one.

It is one thing to know the Bible and understand its message. It is quite another thing to love the Bible and to desire the God revealed in its pages. Christianity is not simply (or primarily) about what we know. It is about *who* we know, Who loves us, and Who we love. Having our affections involved in our faith is not optional. It is not icing on the cake. The cake is not made without them. It is a command: "Take delight in the LORD" (Psalm 37:4). Our affections of love,[36] joy, hope, gratitude, grief, anger, hate, fear, etc., are all meant for use and expression in our worship, our work, and our relationships. Consider the following passages:

Love

- Deuteronomy 6:5: "And you must love the LORD your God with all your heart, all your soul, and all your strength."

- Psalm 31:23: "Love the LORD, all you faithful ones!"

- Matthew 22:37-39: "Jesus replied, 'You must love the Lord your God with all your heart, all your soul, and all your mind.' This is the first and greatest commandment. A second is equally important: 'Love your neighbor as yourself.'"

Joy

- Psalm 37:4: "Take delight in the LORD, and he will give you your heart's desires."

- Psalm 97:12: "May all who are godly be happy in the LORD and praise his holy name!"

- Philippians 4:4: "Always be full of joy in the Lord. I say it again—rejoice!"

Hope

- Psalm 146:5: "But happy are those who have the God of Israel as their helper, whose hope is in the LORD their God."

- Romans 15:13: "So I pray that God, who gives you hope, will keep you happy and full of peace as you believe in him. May you overflow with hope through the power of the Holy Spirit."

- 1 Corinthians 13:13: "There are three things that will endure—faith, hope, and love."

Gratitude

- Psalm 100:4: "Enter his gates with thanksgiving; go into his courts with praise. Give thanks to him and bless his name."

- Colossians 3:15: "And always be thankful."

- Hebrews 12:28: "Since we are receiving a kingdom that cannot be destroyed, let us be thankful and please God by worshiping him with holy fear and awe."

Grief

- Psalm 51:17: "The sacrifice you want is a broken spirit. A broken and repentant heart, O God, you will not despise."

- Isaiah 57:15: "The high and lofty one who inhabits eternity, the Holy One, says this: 'I live in that high and holy place with those whose spirits are contrite and humble. I refresh the humble and give new courage to those with repentant hearts.'"

- Matthew 5:4: "God blesses those who mourn, for they will be comforted."

Hate

- Proverbs 8:13: "All who fear the LORD will hate evil."

- Psalm 97:10: "You who love the LORD, hate evil!"

- Psalm 139:21-22: "O LORD, shouldn't I hate those who hate you? Shouldn't I despise those who resist you? Yes, I hate them with complete hatred, for your enemies are my enemies."

Fear

- Deuteronomy 6:13: "You must fear the LORD your God and serve him."

- Psalm 33:8: "Let everyone in the world fear the LORD, and let everyone stand in awe of him."

- Proverbs 3:7: "Instead, fear the LORD and turn your back on evil."

The more we "think on these things" (Philippians 4:8 KJV) and work at involving our affections in our relationship with and worship of God, the more we will become like Him. To become more forgiving, to become forgiving as Jesus is, we must love what He loves, hate what He hates, grieve with Him when He grieves, hope in what He hopes. We must love mercy the way Jesus loves mercy. A constant hunger and desire for God will move us toward the qualities we need in order to become more forgiving.

2. Proper Self-love

In the *Book of Common Worship* is a prayer that says, "Forgive me, I have not loved others as I have loved myself." The prayer assumes that we really love ourselves the way we should love other people. How do we know this is true? What if we treated other people badly because we did not love ourselves the way we are supposed to? There is a lot of criticism from evangelical circles today saying we are too concerned with ourselves. "We need to stop helping ourselves, satisfying ourselves, and start loving and helping other people," they say. There is one problem with this thinking: If you do not love yourself, if you are not concerned about your own happiness, if you do not have a good, healthy self-image, you cannot love other people the way Jesus commands you to.

The issue is not to stop loving ourselves but to get a proper self-image. We can (and sometimes do) look at ourselves too positively. But it is just as dangerous to look at ourselves too *negatively*. The church has done a fine job of reminding us not to think too highly of ourselves. What we want to do is be sure and not think too negatively about ourselves.

Progress is made the quickest when we are honest about our weaknesses while remaining focused on our strengths. Yes, remember that you are a sinner, but be focused on becoming the redeemed man or woman God wants you to be. Yes, remember the horrible price your sin and rebellion against God cost Him, but focus on the fact that God thought you were worth the price. You deserve hell, but focus on the fact that you are going to heaven. Paul says we should think on whatever is true, honorable, pure, lovely, and admirable (Philippians 4:8). It is our contention that *constantly* dwelling on our shortcomings does not meet the standards Paul has set here for our thoughts.

One of our heroes is a man named David Ring. He was born on October 28, 1953. He was born dead. The time taken in restarting his heart and getting him breathing kept his brain from getting oxygen, and he ended up with cerebral palsy. Several years later his father died. Before he was a teenager, his mother died. He could not talk right. He could not walk right. He was made fun of at school. He wanted to die. And he hated God for making him this way and for taking his parents.

The turning point in his life happened when his sister, who had been caring for him after their mother died, forced him to go to church one Sunday. God found him at that church service. And with his love for Christ came a new love for himself. What a powerful thought! How different would our self-esteem be if we loved ourselves the way God loves us. How does God love you? The simplest we can put it, dear Christian, is that God loves you the same way He loves His Son, Jesus! The Bible says Christians are all sons and daughters of God. Jesus says we are to be one *just as He is one with the Father!* We are in Christ and Christ is in the Father, so we are in the Father. Jesus even says that God loves us just as He loves Christ (John 17:26). What a thought: to love yourself the way God loves you. That is a lot of love! That is positive love.

There is a world of difference between saying, "I am self-centered" and saying, "I love myself." The Bible makes it very clear that one of the results of sin is a self-centered and self-serving nature. But being self-centered and loving yourself are not the same.

Biblical love moves us to be concerned with the happiness of other people. The more truly we love ourselves, the better we will be at loving other people. When a person has trouble loving others, there is almost always an equally bad or worse problem with that person loving himself or herself. By working on a Christlike love for ourselves, we are by default improving and increasing our love to other people.

3. Looking Forward, Not Back

Have you ever heard the term *rubbernecker?* A rubbernecker is what you call the person who is always looking to see the accident on the other side of the highway. We all have been in slow and crawling traffic simply because people who are morbidly curious want to slowly drive by the accident and look back to see as much as they can. There is nothing blocking their way. They are just fixated on looking anywhere but on the road in front of them. Being a rubbernecker slows you down and slows down lots of other people as well.

The highway is not the only place we find rubberneckers. We can be rubberneckers in life, too. Sometimes we get so fixated on the past, things that are behind us, that we stop looking where we are going. Highway rubberneckers are fixated on things that they cannot change and that most of the time are none of their business. When we focus on what happened in the past, we are keeping ourselves from going forward.

Looking forward means accepting that what has happened to us or what we have done is in the past and cannot be changed. It means when dealing with events that happened in the past, we keep our eyes focused on where we want to go. Is stopping to deal with what happened going to help us get to where we are going, or is it going to stop us? We must deal with things in the past in ways that will continue to move us forward until we get back on track.

We must be learning to see things in their big-picture perspective. How will events affect us a week from now, a month from now, a year from now? When we fixate on things, they get bigger to us. By stepping back and looking at the big picture, we can get a better perspective on the situation in relation to everything else. One of the main lessons you learn while taking art lessons is not to get focused on one area of a drawing. When we do that, we almost guarantee that what we focused on will be bigger than it should be and will force us to start over or distort the rest of the picture to compensate for the problem.

In contrast, let us tell you about Virginia. Virginia is a woman who personifies looking forward. Virginia married her high school sweetheart, John. John, however, was not a sweetheart. He was physically abusive. Even when they were dating in high school, he was beating her. Virginia believed she could change him, though, and stayed with him. After more than four years of dating and one year of marriage, Virginia had gotten to the point where, as she described it, "I was so numb from the abuse that John really could not hurt me any more than he had."

During one of these fights, John seemed to realize that there was nothing more he could do to Virginia. So he started to make his way to the crib of their one-year-old daughter. Something rose inside Virginia and, despite all her fears and self-doubt, she stepped in between her daughter and John. "You will never hurt her the way you hurt me!" she cried, and literally pushed him over to the door. Amazingly, stunned by this sudden show of resistance, John left without a fight.

If anyone had a reason to call herself a victim, Virginia did. But Virginia did not see it that way. All through that relationship, she looked to God for strength and direction and comfort. "Why is this person on earth? Why couldn't he change?" she thought. What kept her going was her belief that God was in control. "I just believed there had to be a reason for my experience. Everything happens for a reason. I don't think I would be alive if I did not have that hope."

Virginia did forgive John for what he had done to her. Their marriage, however, did not survive. To this day, very few people know about these dark chapters in her life. Virginia still has to grapple with her past. Nightmares still haunt her. Forgiveness has been a long and painful process. Trust with other men has been a challenge to establish.

But that struggle has not been without fruit. Today, Virginia is a very well-respected and trusted employee for a national telecommunications company. She teaches a "Dress for Success" class every Thursday night at her church. She has a spirit and attitude that wins the respect of her daughter's schoolmates.

While we certainly cannot control everything that happens to us, like Virginia could not, she reminds us that we are in complete control of how we respond to what happens to us. Take responsibility for what you can and learn to live with the reality of what you cannot control.

4. Looking for Good Instead of Problems

One of the cardinal laws of personal relations is this: People thrive under praise and deteriorate under criticism.[37] This idea did not originate in the self-help books such as Dale Carnegie's classic, *How to Win Friends and Influence People*. It is biblical. Consider the following passages: "It is foolish to belittle a neighbor; a person with good sense remains silent" (Proverbs 11:12). "Some people make cutting remarks, but the words of the wise bring healing" (Proverbs 12:18). "Gentle words bring life and health; a deceitful tongue crushes the spirit" (Proverbs 15:4). "Those who love to talk will experience the consequences, for the tongue can kill or nourish life" (Proverbs 18:21).

If we want to be exceptional in our relationships, we have to master this basic principle: People thrive under praise and deteriorate under criticism. Look for the good in other people and praise it. Praise it often. Praise it sincerely. Nothing motivates a person more to respect you and respond to you than honest praise. Nothing brings up our defensiveness faster than criticism. Oswald Chambers writes in *My Utmost for His Highest*,

> Jesus' instructions with regard to judging others is very simply put; He says, "Don't." The average Christian is the most piercingly critical individual known. Criticism is one of the ordinary activities of people, but in the spiritual realm nothing is accomplished by it. The effect of criticism is the dividing up of the strengths of the one being criticized. The Holy Spirit is the only one in the proper position to criticize, and He alone is able to show what is wrong without hurting and wounding. It is impossible to enter into fellowship with God when you are in a critical mood. Criticism serves to make you harsh, vindictive, and cruel, and leaves you with the soothing and flattering idea that you are somehow superior to others. Jesus says that as His disciple you should cultivate a temperament that is never critical. This will not happen quickly but

must be developed over a span of time. You must
constantly beware of anything that causes you to
think of yourself as a superior person....Stop
having a measuring stick for other people. There is
always at least one more fact, which we know
nothing about, in every person's situation....I have
never met a person I could despair of, or lose all
hope for, after discerning what lies in me apart
from the grace of God.

Praise what people are doing right, and you will be amazed
at how fast they learn! Remember, Zacchaeus exceeded all the
requirements of the law by returning four times what he had
stolen and giving away half his wealth to the poor. Surely this
was more than anyone who would rather that Jesus criticized
Zacchaeus could have hoped for. Jesus demonstrated that a
good meal and a smile can do more than years of social ostra-
cizing by a grumbling crowd.

5. Be Looking for Opportunities to Be Gracious

The fifth habit we need to have is the habit of looking for
the opportunity to be gracious. Human nature seems geared to
seek, find, and expose fault for the purpose of criticizing it.
Mark had an opportunity to live out this habit of graciousness
with a co-worker of his one night at the convenience store he
works at. Mark asked his co-worker Jim how he was doing.
"Lousy," Jim replied. Jim then proceeded to tell him about his
week. He was desperately short of cash. He had not eaten that
day. He had hardly any gas left in his car. He was told by his
parents that he should quit working here, get a "real job," quit
college (it was not doing him any good anyway), and no, they
would not loan him 20 dollars for the week until he was paid.
"What's really bad," he continued, "is my parents are strict
Roman Catholics."

Jim was not a dependable employee, and Mark was often left doing much of the work when they shared shifts. Jim was also living at his girlfriend's apartment, which was one of the big reasons Jim's parents were so upset with him. Knowing all this, Mark just listened to Jim and offered him money for gas so he could get home. That was an opportunity to show grace. Hosea 6:6 (NIV) says, "I desire mercy, not sacrifice." Jesus repeats this verse to the Pharisees in the New Testament. That means the verse is important. The situation with his co-worker could easily have been an opportunity for Mark to condemn, but he chose to be gracious.

Graciousness and a forgiving attitude go hand in hand. A gracious spirit is a forgiving spirit. It is interesting that in the Beatitudes mercy comes before purity. Mercy is one of the main ingredients that makes you pure in heart. We often fall into the trap of the Pharisees by majoring on the minors. We focus on rules, obligations, and commands that focus on actions instead of focusing on the attitudes that should go behind the actions. Many of us can do very well at the external actions, but these are not as important as the inner attitudes. For instance, how many of us really want to excel at being poor in spirit, loving our enemies, and not judging other people? Bad attitudes produce bad fruit. Ask yourself, "How does a gracious person think? How can I help this person?" Be sensitive to the needs of other people. Be more concerned about healing them than criticizing them. Be more concerned about being forgiving than being right.

6. Be Optimistic and Positive

It is very hard to be stingy with grace when you are optimistic and positive. Maybe you know someone like Ned. Ned was incredibly negative. Whenever he stopped by a co-worker's desk, he would shake his head and say, "I don't know..." which was his introduction to an extended period of complaining, griping, blaming, and gossiping. People started calling him "Captain Negative."

This guy was a very good worker. He did his job very well—extremely well. But he was soon frustrated that he was not getting the promotions. He felt that everyone was against him. No one was obviously doing their jobs because, if they were, they would have promoted him by now. If he thought you crossed him, you were on his bad list. He finally ended up leaving, angry and frustrated that he had not been promoted.

There was not a person where he worked who was not glad—even relieved—to see him go. Do you know why? Because he was negative. He was not a very gracious or kind person. No one wants to be with a Captain Negative. Grace, forgiveness, goodness, kindness, and mercy are all positive and optimistic by nature. If you want to be forgiving, you need to be a positive, optimistic person.

7. Regular Prayer

Prayer comes easier to some people and harder to others. The more honest way of saying this is that prayer *seems* easier to some people. Prayer takes work. Prayer stays difficult for primarily two reasons: first, when we do not understand what prayer is and what it is for; and second, when we do not know how to go about praying. Let's talk briefly about each of these.

Prayer is one of the key ways we build our relationship with God. It is special because prayer is intimate and personal. In the Bible, God speaks to us through His words to the church in all times and all places. In prayer, God speaks with you one-on-one.

Prayer is not only talking with God, it is also the means by which we are empowered by the Holy Spirit. Prayer works through our supernatural unity with Jesus and the Father through the Holy Spirit. Prayer means spending time with God. It means spending time in His presence. The more time you spend with God, the more clearly you will see things as God sees them.

There are several themes that make up a healthy prayer life. You may be familiar with the acronym ACTS (Adoration, Confession, Thanksgiving, and Supplication) that many people find helpful in focusing on what to pray about. We have added two more categories to the list: Relating and Listening. All six components do not need to be in every prayer. A prayer may only have one or two of these areas, but they should all be regular themes in our prayers in general.

Six Components of Prayer

• *Adoration*—It is natural to praise what we love. We cheer and chant when our favorite team wins the game. When we are in love, we praise our lover in letters, poetry, and by saying things like, "You are just so wonderful!" Praising God is no different, and it is a whole lot more significant.

When we praise God for who He is and what He has done, we feel better! We cannot stay down in the dumps after getting involved in some real heartfelt praise. That is one of the main reasons to praise God—to keep that excitement and awe of Him fresh in our hearts. Praise keeps us on fire. If you don't feel excited about your relationship with Jesus, start making praise a central part of your prayer time.

• *Confession*—Confession is admitting (and repenting!) for our sins against God and other people. It is very clear that we are to make confession a regular part of prayer as we see in the Lord's Prayer, which served as Christ's blueprint for prayer for His disciples.

Confession can be very scary. When we confess, we are admitting that we are at fault. We are admitting failure and taking responsibility for it. It is a very humbling experience to confess our sins.

Confession gives us three powerful advantages that make it worth doing. First, by taking responsibility for our actions, we are taking the first step to stop that particular sin. Second, the power of sin is greatly diminished when it is verbally confessed. We highly recommend having a friend to whom you can confess your personal sins. By letting another person know about your struggle, you literally start to remove the sin's poison from you and throw it out into God's light. Third, being humbled before God, you make the way clear for God's grace to work powerfully to rid you of that sin.

When we go to a doctor, he or she needs to know exactly where it hurts, what it feels like, how deep the wound is, or how serious the infection is. That is often a very humbling and uncomfortable process. But once the doctor knows what is going on, he or she can begin to help in healing. Confession to God is the same as being honest with your doctor about what is ailing you. If you want to get over the pain and struggle of sin and end the discipline and disappointment it brings, you need to confess your sins to God.

• *Thanksgiving*—If you read any number of prayers in the Bible, you will soon realize that thanksgiving is a great part of prayer. Thanksgiving or gratitude is our heartfelt response to God's blessings and grace in our lives. Thanking God acknowledges Him as the Giver, Helper, and Sustainer of our lives. Gratitude glorifies God as the Source for all our good things.

• *Supplication*—This is a very important part of prayer: asking God for help, provision, healing, forgiveness, grace, etc.

It can be for ourselves or for other people. Many Christians do not have a problem including petitions in their prayers. Problems with petition come from it being the dominating theme of our prayers, or from our petitions being virtually the same over and over again.

There is another pitfall to watch for, however: not daring to be bold in asking God for greater things. God's grace and desire to bless us is greater than we could ever imagine! God longs to bless you. Bruce Wilkinson has written a fantastic book on this very subject titled *The Prayer of Jabez*. It cannot be recommended too highly. Get it. Read it and read it again. It is a life-changing book.

Remember what Paul said in Ephesians 3:20: "Now glory be to God! By his mighty power at work within us, he is able to accomplish infinitely more than we would ever dare to ask or hope." Be daring, bold, and expectant when you pray. Prayer is well summarized by Psalm 50:15 where God says, "Trust me in your times of trouble, and I will rescue you, and you will give me glory." We glorify God by confessing that we need Him, and we glorify Him again by praising Him when He provides for that need.

• *Relating*—One of the main areas of prayer is in working on our friendship with God. Prayer is conversation and therefore needs to be *conversational*. It is very important in prayer to talk with God like we would talk to a very close friend (or someone we were wanting to get to know very well). We need to be honest about what we are thinking, feeling and struggling with. We should tell Him what is important to us, what our desires and dreams are. And we should also tell Him about our fears, frustrations, joys, and sorrows. We need to be personal with God.

• *Listening*—Of all the parts of prayer, the most difficult, and therefore the most neglected, is allowing God to have a time to speak to us. That means listening, and it is very hard to listen while our mouth is moving! God may speak clearly in our hearts. Sometimes it is a still, small voice. Sometimes it is a loud and thundering voice. He may speak by bringing thoughts or scriptures to mind. There are many ways He speaks. We must allow God the chance to speak to us. Prayer is conversation, and that means it is a two-way street. Perhaps it would be more correct to say we must give ourselves the chance to hear what God is saying to us. Let's take time to sit and listen to God while we pray. We need to stop doing all the talking.

Ideas on How to Pray

The second thing that often keeps us from praying (or praying effectively) is in not knowing how to pray. For some people, prayer is awkward and unnatural. For others, the problem lies in thinking about prayer as needing to be in a certain form or method. If you struggle with praying at all, the most important key is to start. If prayer seems unnatural, it is because it *is* unnatural. Prayer is as unnatural as forgiveness. Prayer can also seem awkward to us because it takes effort and commitment on our part. Prayer takes work so it feels comfortable.

Start by committing to a time each day to spend time with God and pray. Trying to go from little or no prayer, to a two-hour commitment every morning starting at 4:00 AM is simply setting yourself up for failure. Be *realistic*. Be *simple*. Just set aside five minutes each day *at a specific time* and work from there.

There are a number of methods that are helpful in cultivating and maintaining a productive prayer life. If you are looking for a form or a method of prayer, here are a few ideas that work for all kinds of people:

- *Keep a prayer journal.* Write out your prayers and what you think God is saying back in response. Keep track of when you ask for things and date when God answers your prayers.

- *Imagine yourself sitting with God and talking with Him as you pray.* Having a mental image can be very helpful in creating focus for prayer.

- *Find a place you can go that is comfortable and relaxing to pray.* Have a place that is free from distractions such as the phone, TV, radio, family, roommates, etc. Being alone can help you focus, as well.

- *Join a prayer group or find someone who can be a prayer partner with you.* There is something about praying in a group that makes prayer more dynamic. Having a prayer partner also creates accountability for one another.

Try these different prayer ideas. Many people have done all four at different times and found them all to be very helpful in different ways. Your pastor can probably give you some fresh ideas, too. However you pray, *pray.* The more often you do, the easier it will become and the closer you will get to God and, therefore, the more you will become like Him.

8. Have Mentors from Whom You Can Learn

Having mentors is extremely important. Mentors not only represent the kind of people we want to be and the success we want to achieve, but they also go a step further. They counsel, guide, and direct us to get where we want to go in a given area. We not only want to surround ourselves as much as possible with gracious, forgiving people, but we also want to try to have at least one of them as a mentor. This does not need to be a pastor, but it should be someone we trust and respect. Should there not be a person, do not feel left out, your best mentors can come from books.

If we want to learn how to be forgiving, we should spend time—as much time as we can—with a person or persons we feel are exceptional at being forgiving. We must listen to the way they talk, watch the way they carry themselves, and watch the way they react to difficult situations. What habits do they have? What mannerisms do they have? What characteristics do they have? What kind of attitudes do they have?

We too often get information and advice for personal growth and change from people who are in the same ruts as we are. We need to search for a person who is exceptionally gracious and listen to that individual.

9. Read Books

Why is reading books on this list? Reading changes the way we think. Books present new thoughts, new pictures, and new awarenesses to our minds. We constantly have to be feeding our minds what we need to become who we want to be.

The world is full of thoughts, attitudes, and actions that discourage us from being gracious and forgiving. To stay forgiving, to grow more forgiving, one of the best ways to counter these thoughts, attitudes, and actions is through reading. What kind of books? The Bible (of course), biographies, histories, positive books, books on Christian living and self-improvement, even fiction…all types of books.

Make reading a habit. Read a little every day, even 10 or 15 minutes. Keep a book in the bathroom. Read your Bible every day. Do not concern yourself with reading a certain number of passages each day right now. Just read *something* every day.

Reading may be something that you vowed never to do again after high school or college. You may not even know where to start reading again, so we have included a list of books (pages 155–158) that we have read and enjoyed and grown and learned from. Ask your pastor for ideas. Go to your local bookstore and browse around, but start reading.

10. Avoid Things That Promote Inappropriate Hate, Anger, and Negativity

This last habit is one of the most difficult but is also one of the most important. You not only need to find positive, gracious people to hang around, but you also have to distance yourself from negative people. You *must* distance yourself from negative people and things. This could require major change on your part. It may require you to look for some new friends. It may require you to think about your own attitudes toward life.

It is a fact that negative thought patterns and attitudes make you feel tired, depressed, ineffective, doubtful, slow, and even prone to health problems. Negative people, thoughts, and stimuli actually drain your energy. One of the most positive things you can do to stay healthy and energetic (not to mention to promote forgiveness) is, as much as possible, to avoid anyone or anything that promotes *inappropriate* hate, anger, or negativity in your life.

Now we need to make one thing very clear here: we will never be able to cut out all of the negative people and influences in our lives. That is not possible this side of heaven. In fact, we shared in chapter 14 that God uses our problems, challenges, heartaches, and stress to help us become more like Christ. Read these words from Charles Spurgeon.

> Our heavenly Father sends us frequent troubles to try our faith. If our faith be worth anything, it will stand the test. Gilt is afraid of fire, but gold is not: the paste gem dreads to be touched by the diamond, but the true jewel fears no test. It is a poor faith which can only trust God when friends are true, the body full of health, and the business profitable; but that is true faith which holds by the Lord's faithfulness when friends are gone, when the body is sick, when spirits are depressed, and the light of our Father's countenance is hidden. A faith which can say, in the direst trouble, "Though he slay me, yet will I trust in him," is heaven-born faith.[39]

God wants you to become like Christ. And He uses all your troubles, sins, mistakes, heartaches, and failures to do it.

What we are talking about are the negative influences that we *choose* to allow ourselves to be continually and habitually influenced by. For instance, when you talk with people who are very confident, positive, upbeat, gracious, and loving you will often find that they have given up or avoid as much as possible the following things:

- TV in general
- Soap operas
- Watching the news
- Reading newspapers
- Certain musical styles or groups
- Arguing with other people

- Gossip and people who gossip
- Finger-pointing and blaming
- Criticism, even positive criticism
- Chronically negative people
- Trashy books
- Movies that promote negative patterns of behavior or people

If you really want to become more of a forgiving person, you will need to think seriously about giving up or avoiding as much as possible the things on this list. If we want to be a forgiving person, you must promote whenever possible the people and things in your life that will pull you in that direction and minimize the influence of the people and things that are pulling you in the other direction.

Summary
and Conclusion

THE MOST COMMON PROBLEMS with forgiveness come from removing its Godward axis. It is like trying to get the kitchen faucet to work when the water has been shut off at the pipe. It does not matter how good the faucet is or how hard you work it; you are not going to get any water until you open the valve at the pipe under the sink. The same is true with forgiveness. If you want it to work, it is not enough to have a working faucet; the water needs to be turned on at the pipe.

A truly biblical understanding of vertical forgiveness requires that we understand the seriousness of sin and the awful reality of God's holiness. As sinners apart from Christ, we are in a hopeless situation before our holy and righteous God, deserving only an infinite punishment. While we could do nothing to change this, God offers forgiveness to us through the atoning death of Jesus Christ, His Son. In Christ's death, God looked at Him as our Substitute and allowed Jesus

151

to take the punishment that we deserved by putting our sin on Himself. God forgives us by uniting us to Christ through His Spirit by pronouncing us justified—free from guilt before the law—and then by giving us new hearts and actually changing us throughout our life into Christ's likeness.

Horizontal forgiveness, powered by vertical forgiveness, allows us to look at people and forgive them through the cross of Christ. The cross for the forgiver reveals that the sin against them was punished at the cross, so the anger and desire for justice are both satisfied, making continuing in relationship possible. The cross for the offender provides the release of guilt because he sees his sin was punished there with Jesus as his Substitute. He also sees that the forgiver (along with God) has accepted this Substitute and has released his or her anger and cry for justice to the cross.

In reading this book, you have taken a step toward living a life marked by gracious forgiveness. Now you are ready to take the next step: learning to do what you know. You have shown you have the will to prepare. Now it is time to get out there and start practicing forgiveness. Do not worry about doing everything right. Just start doing!

The Church (and the world) is in desperate need of people who know, understand, and (most importantly) practice forgiveness. Make a commitment to God. Make a promise to God to do whatever you need to do to become the most forgiving and gracious person you can be. It does not matter where you are starting from. It does not matter how many problems or challenges you have had with forgiveness up to this point in your life. God can and will take you from your point A—wherever that might be—to point B, to being a person of whom others will say, "There is a gracious and forgiving person."

Become that person. With God's help, you can be.

Dear reader, this little book was mainly intended for the edification of believers, but if you are still unsaved, we are concerned for you, and would like to say something that would be helpful to you. Open your Bible, and read this story of the lepers [2 Kings 7], and note their position which is similar to yours. If you remain where you are, you must perish; if you go to Jesus you will live. "Nothing ventured nothing gained" is the old proverb, and in your case the venture is not great. If you still sit in sullen despair, no one can pity you when your ruin comes; but if you were to die seeking mercy, if such a thing were possible, you would be the object of universal sympathy. None escape who refuse to look to Jesus; but you know others are saved who believe in Him, for certain of your own friends and neighbors have received mercy. So why not you? Why not taste and see the Lord is merciful? To perish is so awful that if you could only clutch at a straw, the instinct of self-preservation should lead you to stretch out your hand. We want to assure you, as from the Lord, that if you seek Him you will find Him. Jesus casts none out who come to Him. You shall not perish if you trust Him; on the contrary, you shall find treasure far richer than what the poor lepers gathered in Syria's deserted camp. May the Holy Spirit embolden you to go at once, and you shall not believe in vain. Then when you are saved, share the good news with others. Do not hold back; tell your friends at church first, and join with them in fellowship; let the watchman of the city, the pastor, be informed of your discovery, and then proclaim the good news in every place. May the Lord God save you before the sun goes down this day.

SPURGEON, *MORNING AND EVENING*, MARCH 13

Recommended Reading

You are the same today as you will be in five years except for two things: the people you meet and the books you read.

THE MOST IMPORTANT BOOKS you will ever discover are the 66 books in the Bible. "So then faith cometh by hearing, and hearing by the word of God" (Romans 10:17 KJV). "Study to show thyself approved unto God, a workman that needeth not be ashamed, rightly dividing the word of truth" (2 Timothy 2:15 KJV).

The most important person you will ever meet is Jesus Christ, the Son of God. "He that hath the Son hath life; and he that hath not the Son of God hath not life" (1 John 5:12 KJV). "And it shall come to pass, that whosoever shall call on the name of the Lord shall be saved" (Acts 2:21 KJV).

There are hundreds of great books that will bless your life. Here are a few that have blessed our lives.

Christian Living

Freedom of Forgiveness, David Augsburger
Half Time, Bob Buford
Intimacy with the Almighty, Charles Swindoll
Knowing God, J. I. Packer
Let Go, François Fénelon
Religious Affections, Jonathan Edwards
The Cost of Discipleship, Dietrich Bonhoeffer
The Passion, John Piper
The Purpose-Driven Life, Rick Warren
What's So Amazing About Grace? Philip Yancey

Christian Theology

Basic Christianity, John Stott
Bondage of the Will, Martin Luther
Mere Christianity, C.S. Lewis
Prayer, O. Hallesby
Renewing Your Mind, R.C. Sproul
The Case for Christ, Lee Strobel
The Names of Jesus, A.B. Simpson
The Normal Christian Life, Watchman Nee
What Jesus Means to Me, H.W. Gockel
What the Bible Is All About, Henrietta Mears

Inspirational

Greatest Miracle in the World, Og Mandino
How They Found Christ in Their Own Words, Bill Freeman
How to Win Over Worry, John Haggai

See You at the Top, Zig Ziglar
The Power of Crying Out, Bill Gothard
The Power of Positive Thinking, Norman Vincent Peale
The Ultimate Gift, Jim Stovall
They Found the Secret, V. Raymond Edman
We Are the Beloved, Ken Blanchard
Why I Believe, D. James Kennedy

Personal Growth

Five Pillars of Leadership, Paul J. Meyers
How to Win Friends and Influence People, Dale Carnegie
Life Is Tremendous, Charlie Jones
Motivational Classics, 1. As a Man Thinketh, 2. Kingship of Self Control, 3. Acres of Diamonds, Executive Books
Running with the Giants, John Maxwell
Ten Things I Learned from Bill Porter, Shelby Brady
The Pillars of Leadership, David J. Vaughn
The Success System That Never Fails, W. Clement Stone
The University of Success, Og Mandino
You and Your Network, Fred Smith

Biographies and Autobiographies

Eric Liddell: Something Greater Than Gold, Janet and Geoff Benge
Jeanne Guyon: An Autobiography
Daws: The Story of Daws Trotman, Betty Lee Skinner
The Autobiography of George Mueller
My Life for the Poor, Mother Teresa
Confessions, St. Augustine
Dream Big, Henrietta Mears
Fled from Darkness: Booker T. Washington, George Grant
Jonathan Edwards: A Life, George Marsden
Treasure of Clay, Fulton Sheen

Devotionals

Dare to Journey with Henri Nouwen
Day by Day with the Early Church Fathers
Morning and Evening, C.H. Spurgeon
My Utmost for His Highest, Oswald Chambers
Quiet Moments with God, Lloyd John Ogilvie
Resist the Powers with Jacques Ellul, Charles Ringma
Streams in the Desert, Mrs. Charles E. Cowman
The Best of Andrew Murray on Prayer
The One Year Book of Hymns by Robert K. Brown
The Best of A.W. Tozer

Study Guide

The Best-kept Secret: Forgiveness

> You must make allowance for each other's faults and forgive the person who offends you. Remember, the Lord forgave you, so you must forgive others (Colossians 3:13).

1. Do you find that people are confused about how to make forgiveness work? If so, what do you think are some of the reasons forgiveness is so hard to do or to accept?

2. Which of the four groups of people who struggle with forgiveness do you identify with? What is one of your biggest struggles with forgiveness?

3. Do you think forgiveness is a secret? Why or why not?

4. What is the most important question about forgiveness to which you want the answer? Why is that important to you? What are the consequences of not getting the answer to that question?

5. Why should we be interested in what the Bible has to say about forgiveness?

Chapter 1—The Words Behind Forgiveness

> O Lord, you are so good, so ready to forgive, so full of unfailing love for all who ask your aid (Psalm 86:5).

1. Why is knowing the meaning of the Greek and Hebrew words we translate as "forgive" important to understanding the biblical concept of forgiveness?

2. Which Greek or Hebrew word helped you understand forgiveness in a way you had not thought of yet?

3. Using the definitions for the Greek and Hebrew words given in this chapter, write what you think would be a good working definition of *forgiveness*.

Chapter 2—Passages Where the Word Is Used

> If you forgive those who sin against you, your heavenly Father will forgive you. But if you refuse to forgive others, your Father will not forgive your sins (Matthew 6:14-15).

1. How do you interpret Matthew 6:14-15? Is our forgiveness dependent on how well we forgive other people, or is our forgiveness of other people a proof that we really have been forgiven? What are the reasons for your answer?

2. What is the difference between apologizing and repenting?

3. What do you think was Jesus' reason for telling the parable of the unforgiving servant?

4. Why do you think Jesus forgave the paralytic in Luke 5:18-26 before He physically healed him? What does Jesus teach us about forgiveness by doing what He did in that story?

Chapter 3—Passages Where the Concept Is Used

> Under the old system, the blood of goats and bulls and the ashes of a young cow could cleanse people's bodies from ritual defilement. Just think how much more the blood of Christ will purify our hearts from deeds that lead to death so that we can worship the living God. For by the power of the eternal Spirit, Christ offered himself to God as a perfect sacrifice for our sins. That is why he is the one who mediates the new covenant between God and people, so that all who are invited can receive the eternal inheritance God has promised them. For Christ died to set them free from the penalty of the sins they had committed under that first covenant (Hebrews 9:13-15).

1. What are the benefits of offering forgiveness before a person repents? Is doing that harder than waiting for repentance?

2. What are the consequences of not offering forgiveness?

3. Why is sacrifice needed before forgiveness can be offered?

4. Jesus' death is referred to as a sacrifice throughout the New Testament. What parallels can you draw between Old Testament sacrifices and Jesus' death on the cross?

Chapter 4—The Importance of Seeing the Big Picture

> Instead, you must worship Christ as Lord of your life. And if you are asked about your Christian hope, always be ready to explain it. But you must do this in a gentle and respectful way. Keep your conscience clear. Then if people speak evil against you, they will be ashamed when they see what a good life you live because you belong to Christ (1 Peter 3:15-16).

1. What is "theology"?

2. Why does theology need to be rational to be relational?

3. Does Christianity offer a realistic picture of the world to you? Does Christianity make sense of your experiences? Why or why not?

4. Which of the four tests for a reasonable faith is most important to you? Why?

Chapter 5—Why We Need Forgiveness

> No one has real understanding; no one is seeking
> God (Romans 3:11).

1. Most people think that people are basically good but do some bad things. The Bible teaches that people are basically bad but try to do good things. Which view makes more sense in your experience with people?

2. The greater our obligation to love, honor, and obey a person, the more serious the consequences will be when we fail to meet that obligation. Do you agree with that statement? Why or why not?

3. Why is offense against God so serious to Him?

Chapter 6—How God Made Forgiveness Possible

> Yet now God in his gracious kindness declares us
> not guilty. He has done this through Christ Jesus,
> who has freed us by taking away our sins. For God
> sent Jesus to take the punishment for our sins and
> to satisfy God's anger against us. We are made right
> with God when we believe that Jesus shed his
> blood, sacrificing his life for us (Romans 3:24-25).

1. Justice is the forerunner of forgiveness. How does this idea compare to the common understanding that forgiveness is "just forgetting about it"?

2. Why is it important that Jesus did not simply volunteer to die, but volunteered also to receive God's punishment for sin?

3. Why do you think Jesus cried out on the cross, "My God, my God, why have you forsaken me?"

4. What are some of the promises God has given us that we can be sure of because Jesus prayed this prayer on the cross: "My God, my God, why have you forsaken me?"

Chapter 7—Why God Made Forgiveness Possible

Let them boast in this alone: that they truly know me and understand that I am the LORD who is just and righteous, whose love is unfailing, and that I delight in these things. I, the LORD, have spoken (Jeremiah 9:24).

1. What is the relationship between grace and mercy? How are they alike? How are they different?

2. What are the benefits of believing in the sovereignty of God? Why are those benefits important? What would the consequences be without those benefits?

3. Why does God need to punish sin? Why can He not just overlook it?

Chapter 8—What God's Forgiveness Means

And so, dear brothers and sisters, we can boldly enter heaven's Most Holy Place because of the blood of Jesus. This is the new, life-giving way that Christ has opened up for us through the sacred curtain, by means of his death for us. And since we have a great High Priest who rules over God's people, let us go right into the presence of God, with true hearts fully trusting him. For our evil consciences have been sprinkled with Christ's blood to make us clean, and our bodies have been washed with pure water (Hebrews 10:19-22).

1. What is the relationship between being forgiven and being justified before God?

2. Which of the five aspects of God's forgiveness means the most to you? Why?

3. Which of the five aspects of God's forgiveness is the hardest for you to understand or accept? Why?

Chapter 9—The Fruit of God's Forgiveness

There was a time when some of you were just like that, but now your sins have been washed away, and you have been set apart for God. You have been made right with God because of what the Lord Jesus Christ and the Spirit of our God have done for you (1 Corinthians 6:11).

1. Discuss how justification and sanctification are related. How are they similar? How are they different?

2. Why do we still need to ask for forgiveness from God once we have been justified?

3. Are your eyes shut to the forgiveness God has already given you? In what ways? How can you overcome that roadblock to realizing God's forgiveness?

Chapter 10—How God's Forgiveness Is Applied

> As the sun went down and it became dark, Abram saw a smoking firepot and a flaming torch pass between the halves of the carcasses. So the LORD made a covenant with Abram that day and said, "I have given this land to your descendants, all the way from the border of Egypt to the great Euphrates River" (Genesis 15:17-18).

1. What is the foundation of our union with Jesus?

2. Why is it important that God takes all the responsibility in making sure our union with Jesus is secure? What are the consequences if this were not the case?

3. Why is unity with Jesus through the Holy Spirit necessary for us to both receive and offer forgiveness?

4. What are some of the ways in which we acknowledge our unity with Jesus through the Holy Spirit?

Chapter 11—What Our Forgiveness of Others Means

> If you forgive those who sin against you, your heavenly Father will forgive you. But if you refuse to forgive others, your Father will not forgive your sins (Matthew 6:14-15).

1. The starting point for understanding how we forgive is in understanding that we *by ourselves* have neither the right nor the ability to forgive anybody of anything. Why is this important to understanding how to effectively forgive people?

2. The biblical idea of forgiveness is very Trinitarian; that is, God the Father, Jesus the Son, and God the Holy Spirit each play a very important role in giving forgiveness. What role does each member of the Trinity play in making forgiveness possible?

3. What are the benefits of offering forgiveness? Is it right for a person to be motivated to forgive because of the benefits forgiveness offers? Why or why not?

4. The Bible is very clear that God needs to forgive along with us if our forgiveness is going to have any lasting meaning. What are the implications of this? Could this be a reason why so many people have such a hard time giving or receiving forgiveness?

Chapter 12—What Forgiveness Is Not

> So we praise God for the wonderful kindness he has poured out on us because we belong to his dearly loved Son. He is so rich in kindness that he purchased our freedom through the blood of his Son, and our sins are forgiven (Ephesians 1:6-7).

1. Which of the myths about forgiveness have led to the most trouble in your life or in the life of someone you know?

2. What is the difference between being guilty and feeling guilty?

3. Why do guilt feelings or feelings of anger often still remain after we have been forgiven or offered forgiveness?

Does the fact that we still feel those emotions mean our forgiveness was not genuine or that we were not forgiven? Why or why not?

Chapter 13—Forgiveness Is Not Optional

Forgive as the Lord forgave you (Colossians 3:13).

1. Why should we as Christians be gladly willing to forgive other people?

2. What is the purpose of confession? How is it related to forgiveness?

3. Who do you think better fits your current understanding of forgiveness: Valjean or Javert? Why?

4. Albert Einstein said, "The height of insanity is doing the same thing and expecting a different outcome." Why do we so often use criticism to promote change when it is such an ineffective method of bringing it about?

Chapter 14—Forgiving Yourself

Create in me a clean heart, O God. Renew a right spirit within me. Do not banish me from your presence, and don't take your Holy Spirit from me. Restore to me again the joy of your salvation, and make me willing to obey you. Then I will teach your ways to sinners, and they will return to you. Forgive me for shedding blood, O God who saves; then I will joyfully sing of your forgiveness. Unseal my lips, O LORD, that I may praise you. You would not be pleased with sacrifices, or I would bring them. If I brought you a burnt offering, you would not accept it. The sacrifice you want is a broken spirit. A broken and repentant heart, O God, you will not despise (Psalm 51:10-17).

1. Why do you think the idea of forgiving yourself is so popular today in light of the fact that the Bible does not discuss forgiving yourself at all?

2. Why is taking responsibility for our actions necessary in confronting our guilt?

3. Do you think there is a difference between discipline and punishment? Why or why not? Does God still punish Christians today? Why or why not?

Chapter 15—When Anger Keeps Us from Forgiving

Get rid of all bitterness, rage, anger, harsh words, and slander, as well as all types of malicious behavior. Instead, be kind to each other, tender-hearted, forgiving one another, just as God through Christ has forgiven you (Ephesians 4:31-32).

1. What are some ways in which we can discern if our feelings of anger are healthy or not?

2. Do you think it is important that anger is part of the image of God in us? Why or why not?

3. How does forgiveness address the anger of the forgiving person?

Chapter 16—When Conscience Keeps Us from Forgiving

> Two men went to the Temple to pray. One was a Pharisee, and the other was a dishonest tax collector. The proud Pharisee stood by himself and prayed this prayer: "I thank you, God, that I am not a sinner like everyone else, especially like that tax collector over there! For I never cheat, I don't sin, I don't commit adultery, I fast twice a week, and I give you a tenth of my income." But the tax collector stood at a distance and dared not even lift his eyes to heaven as he prayed. Instead, he beat his chest in sorrow, saying, "O God, be merciful to me, for I am a sinner." I tell you, this sinner, not the Pharisee, returned home justified before God. For the proud will be humbled, but the humble will be honored (Luke 18:10-14).

1. Are there times when forgiveness is not warranted? Do we sometimes think forgiveness is not possible to rationalize our lack of desire to be gracious? How can you forgive and still give or face consequences?

2. Why is it beneficial to respond to situations rather than to react to them? What are the difficulties in doing so? How can you become better at creating a habit of responding to hurt, offense, or crisis, instead of reacting to it?

3. What is the difference between "compassionate righteousness" and "judgmental righteousness"? Why is one better than the other? How can you tell the difference?

Ten Habits that Promote Forgiveness

> So make every effort to apply the benefits of these promises to your life. Then your faith will produce a life of moral excellence. A life of moral excellence leads to knowing God better. Knowing God leads to self-control. Self-control leads to patient endurance, and patient endurance leads to godliness. Godliness leads to love for other Christians, and finally you will grow to have genuine love for everyone. The more you grow like this, the more you will become productive and useful in your knowledge of our Lord Jesus Christ (2 Peter 1:5-9).

1. Why is what we think important to how we act?

2. Write down three reasons why it is important to you to change your thoughts, attitudes, and actions so you can be a more forgiving person. Why are these reasons important to you?

3. How do our habits positively or negatively influence our desire to forgive? What habits can you start to change right away to help you become a more forgiving person? What steps will you commit to do that this week?

4. Why is cultivating a delight for God so important in growing into a more forgiving person? List three things you can do this week to grow your delight in God.

5. Do you know of anyone whom you would say is very gracious and forgiving? Write down their names and ask one of them if they would be willing to mentor you in that area.

6. Right before this study guide is a list of recommended books that have helped us in our growing up in Christ. Make a commitment to growing through reading by picking a book off our list and starting to read it this week.

Notes

1. *Kaphar* is used only three times in the Old Testament with the meaning of forgiveness (Deuteronomy 21:8; Psalm 78:38; and Jeremiah 18:23).

2. *Nasa* is used to mean forgiveness 15 times throughout the Old Testament.

3. This is the primary word used for forgiveness in the Old Testament. *Sallach* is used 25 times, more than the other two words combined.

4. *Apoluo* is used once in Luke 6:37. Secondary definitions for this word include the ideas of letting go, dismissing, and divorcing.

5. *Charisomai* is used a total of 12 times in Luke and throughout Paul's letters. Further uses of the word include the idea of being very gracious to one another.

6. *Aphami* is the most-often–used word in the New Testament for forgiveness, being used 15 times as a noun and 40 times as a verb. In other places it has the meaning of leaving, giving up, abandoning, and tolerating.

7. William Hendricksen, *Luke* (Grand Rapids, MI: Baker, 1978), p. 301.

8. Leon Morris, *Luke* (Grand Rapids, MI: InterVarsity Press, 1988), p. 130. "If he can do the one he can do the other."

9. Roger T. Beckwith, *Sacrifice in the Bible* (Grand Rapids, MI: Baker Book House, 1995), p. 34. Cited hereafter as *Sacrifice*.

10. *Sacrifice*, p. 36.

11. I am indebted to Ronald Nash and his book *Faith and Reason* (Grand Rapids, MI: Zondervan, 1988), specifically chapter 4 for the following four points.

12. François Fénelon, *Let Go* (New Kensington, PA: Whitaker House, 1973), p. 36.

13. Jonathan Edwards, *The Works of Jonathan Edwards*, vol. 19, M.X. Lesser ed. (New Haven, CT: Yale University Press, 2001), p. 342. "A crime is more or less heinous, according as we are under greater or less obligations to the contrary. This is self evident; because it is herein that the criminalness or faultiness of anything consists, that it is contrary to what we are obliged or bound to, or what ought to be in us. So the faultiness of one being hating another, is in proportion to his obligation to love him. The crime of one being despising and casting contempt on another, is proportionally more or less heinous, as he was under more or less obligations to honor him. The fault of disobeying another, is greater or less, as anyone is under greater or less obligations to obey him….But God is infinitely lovely…infinitely honorable…[and] His authority over us is infinite….So that a sin against God, being a violation of infinite obligations, must be a crime infinitely heinous, and so deserving infinite punishment. Nothing is more agreeable to the commonsense of mankind."

14. Oswald Chambers, *My Utmost for His Highest* (Grand Rapids, MI: Discovery House Press, 1992), from November 20 reading. Hereafter cited as "Chambers."

15. *Sacrifice*, p. 17.

16. Gordon J. Wenham, *The Book of Leviticus* (Grand Rapids, MI: Eerdmans, 1979), p. 62. Hereafter cited as "Wenham."

17. *Sacrifice*, p. 28.

18. Wenham, p. 57. "It propitiates God's wrath against sin."

19. Matthew 26:36-46; Mark 14:32-42; and Luke 22:40-46.

20. Matthew 27:46.

21. Philip Yancey, *What's So Amazing About Grace?* (Grand Rapids, MI: Zondervan, 1997), p. 45.

22. R.C. Sproul, *Chosen By God* (Wheaton, IL: Tyndale House, 1986), pp. 26-27.

23. Gerhard Kittel and Gerhard Friedrich, *Theological Dictionary of the New Testament: Abridged in One Volume*, trans. Geoffrey W. Bromiley (Grand Rapids, MI: Eerdmans, 1985), pp. 589-90.

24. Chambers, November 19 reading.

25. Chambers, December 8 reading.

26. Chambers, November 20 reading.

27. Chambers, December 8 reading.

28. David Augsburger, *The Freedom of Forgiveness: Revised and Expanded* (Chicago: Moody Press, 1988), p. 19. "Freedom, the rush of God's strength, which brings forgiveness, gives in turn the ability to forgive."

29. The Bible does not speak of horizontal forgiveness between persons where vertical forgiveness does not exist. This seems to be the clear deduction of passages such as 1 Samuel 15:26; Psalm 51:4; Jeremiah 11:14; 14:11-12; John 17:12; and Romans 14:23. In these passages, forgiveness is not possible because the forgiveness of God is not extended to the offending persons. This point is, however, debated. Time does not permit me to say more than I already have.

30. Victor Hugo, *Les Misérables* (New York, NY: Random House), p. 89. Hereafter cited as *Les Misérables*.

31. Chambers, April 30 reading.

32. The word translated here as "punishes" is the Greek word for *scourging*. The meaning of the word in the context of verses 5-11 is clearly that sometimes God's discipline can seem very severe to us. There is therefore no reason to understand "punishes" in this passage to be referring to paying the legal penalty for sin that we have been forgiven of in Christ.

33. Chambers, February 17 reading.

34. Ibid.

35. I am indebted to Jonathan Edwards for this discussion on affections. This was the theme of his book *A Treatise Concerning Religious Affections*, which is considered a spiritual classic.

36. C.S. Lewis, *Mere Christianity* (New York: Simon & Schuster, 1996), pp. 105-06.

37. There is a very commonly held notion in some Christian circles that love is not an affection but is simply a choice or a decision. I do not think this idea is biblically supported, nor do I think it is what any of us mean when we say we love something. To read more on this point of view, the book I recommend is John Piper's *Desiring God*.

38. Dale Carnegie, *How to Win Friends and Influence People*, revised ed. (New York: Simon & Schuster, 1981), p. 42. "In our interpersonal relationships we should never forget that all our associates are human beings and hunger for appreciation. It is the legal tender that all souls enjoy," p. 59. "Any fool can complain, condemn and criticize—and most fools do. But it takes character and self-control to be understanding and forgiving."

39. Charles Spurgeon, *Morning and Evening*. October 7th reading.

Other Good
Harvest House Reading

FORGIVE AND LOVE AGAIN
by *John Nieder and Thomas M. Thompson*

With over 80,000 copies sold since it was originally released in 1991, this helpful guide deals with forgiveness in a variety of settings: family, workplace relationships, friendships, and extended family relationships.

HOW TO GET ALONG WITH DIFFICULT PEOPLE
by *Florence Littauer*

Unique insights into dealing with the difficult personalities we all encounter at home or work. This updated, expanded edition of a classic provides fresh direction, encouragement, and skills for those in need of help with a difficult person.

A WOMAN'S ANSWER TO ANGER
by *Annie Chapman*

Annie's story of her struggle with anger will help others learn how to conquer intense emotions, negative words, and angry actions. Readers will discover how to gain control and fix problems created by anger.

GETTING ANGER UNDER CONTROL
by *Neil T. Anderson and Rich Miller*

Whether horrific enough to grab headlines or minor enough to cause arguments with family and friends, uncontrolled anger steals peace, joy, and trust. Here, readers get clear, biblical methods for keeping anger in its place.

BECOMING WHO GOD INTENDED
by *David Eckman*

Whether you realize it or not, your imagination is filled with *pictures* of reality. The Bible indicates these pictures reveal your true "heart beliefs"—the beliefs that actually shape your everyday feelings and reactions to other people, to life's circumstances, and to God. When you allow God's Spirit to build new, *biblical* pictures in your heart and imagination, you will be able to accept God's acceptance of you in Christ, break free of negative emotions and habitual sin...and finally experience the life God the Father has always intended for you.

HARVEST HOUSE
PUBLISHERS